ACKNOWLEDGEMENTS

I AM PLEASED to be able to express my most sincere thanks to **Tim Phillips** and to **Adrian Cleaton:** to Tim for bringing his enterprising and highly imaginative qualities to bear on creating his own stylish visual world. These original concepts immediately took their place as an essential part of the book — lively, expressive, unforgettable, they add a valuable new dimension to it. And to Adrian for the patient use of his computer skills in blending the music, text and charts needed on these pages. His musical background and training have enabled him to plan and achieve this precise, detailed layout, which is both extremely pleasing to the eye and vital to a clear understanding of the subject-matter. *Big Dots and Little Dots* has benefited greatly from the cooperation of both these experts. Thanks also to **Alex Law**, a grade 6 cello student, for making time to look through the pages in proof form.

It is always a pleasure to work with **Jackie** and **Gary Martin** of **IMPRINT** and to know I can rely on them and their speedy and efficient team for an attractive, professional production.

My husband Stephen has always had positive faith in this project. A writer himself, he well appreciates the essential need for quiet and solitude. His unselfish encouragement of my long hours of work – which he rewarded at intervals with cups of tea or glasses of gin and tonic – has enabled me to enjoy the process of writing this book and to achieve its completion. I am so grateful to him for his help.

Hilary Tunnicliffe
Spring 2004

Big Dots and Little Dots

Music Theory up to 5th Grade

Hilary Tunnicliffe

Clairmont Press
2004

Published by
Clairmont Press uk

Clairmont CLUN
Shropshire SY7 8JA

Illustrations by Tim Phillips
Music manuscript, typesetting and design
by Adrian Cleaton

Printed by IMPRINT, Newtown, Powys

ISBN 0 9544779 0 1

ISMN M9002096 3 4

for

Luba Mai

CONTENTS

Big Dots and Little Dots provides in one book a reliable framework of musical theory to a limited standard and for students of varied ages. Learning abilities vary greatly and not necessarily by age; musical concepts which quickly appear logical and simple to some will take longer for others to grasp. The need for clear thinking and memory work soon becomes apparent; for this the study of music theory is a very good training.

* The factual material in *Big Dots and Little Dots* has been arranged in six sections, followed by practice questions and exercises.

* The *Starters* section is fun, and simple enough for 8 to 9-year-olds. It can obviously be skipped over by more advanced students.

* The headings of the next five sections indicate their contents.

  Sections 2-5 run parallel rather than follow on in order of difficulty. The material in them is basic and essential for general theory work.

  Section 6 covers further aspects of GCSE and Grade 5 syllabus requirements.

  The youngest students should select the simplest parts of each section and try the easiest questions and exercises. Understanding will develop gradually.

The various **charts** in the book have been very carefully planned and repay equally careful study.

With the help of *Big Dots and Little Dots* —
parents or grandparents aiming to help young beginners or Grade 5 theory candidates can refresh their own — possibly sketchy – recollections of school music theory

classroom music teachers will be able to present groups of students up to GCSE with the basic facts of music theory, analysis, creative work, etc.

instrumental teachers will find handy explanations and practice exercises for the grade (up to 5) syllabus requirements

interested adults – quite apart from exams – will find the book a useful reference work for their bookshelves.

Hilary Tunnicliffe, LRAM, GRSM

Spring 2004

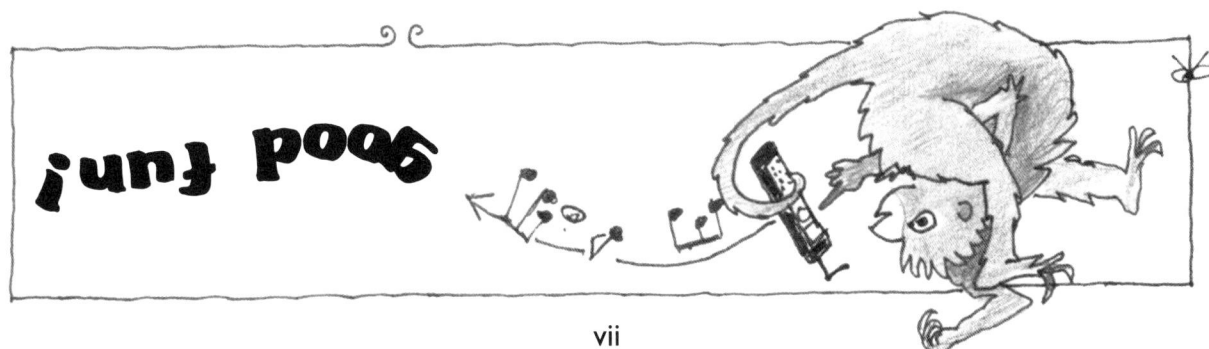

THE LAYOUT OF A KEYBOARD

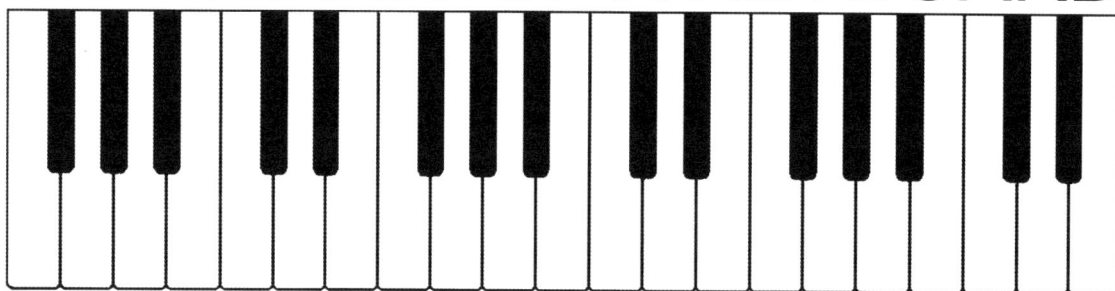

Whichever instrument you play, when learning to write music it's helpful to be able to name the notes on a piano.

- find each block of two black keys; the *white* key between them is **D**.
- on the *left* of **D** is **C**, on the *right* of **D** is **E**.
- on the left in front of **C** come **A** and **B**; after **E** on the right come **F** and **G**.
- these 7 letter-names are repeated across the piano from left to right.
- write the letter names neatly in pencil on the picture above
- the black keys, in blocks of two or three, sound half tones (called semitones) between the white keys
- if there are no black keys, the next door white keys sound the semitones

THE SOUNDS OF THE BLACK AND WHITE KEYS

- black keys take their names from the white keys beside them
- they have two names each: *flats* if they lower the sounds on their right, *sharps* if they raise the sounds on their left

Example

The black note between C and D

- to raise the sound of C it's called C sharp
- to lower the sound of D it's called D flat

KEYBOARD

PITCH

RANGE

As the left hand moves away from the centre of the keyboard the sounds gradually become lower and more resonant.
As the right hand moves away from the centre of the keyboard the sounds gradually become too high to sing. . . . .

. . . . . . and next — a story about those two monkeys —

viii

Monkey Business

or **How the music lines got their names**

Once upon a time there were two young monkeys. They lived with other monkeys in a big cage in a big town zoo. Their names were **Ace** and **Gib** (sounds like Jib). Ace was slightly smaller than Gib; the keepers called him Ace because he was always ace at everything. He was the fastest runner and the most daring jumper, and the greatest show-off — he thought he was the cleverest monkey in the universe.

Gib was a female monkey. She was very friendly and loved jabbering and chattering away to the visitors. The children used to say that her real name was Gibidi-eff, because when they called out to her, "What's your name?" she would chatter *'Gibbi-di-eff – gibbi-di-eff – gib-gib-gib – gibbidee – gibbidee-eff-eff – gibbidee– gib-eff-eff-eff –"* Every time someone called "What's your name?" she would jabber the same answer. She made the children laugh — both the little monkeys were great favourites.

On the cage floor were strewn piles of hay. Ace and Gib loved playing in it, tossing it about and sliding up and down and hiding in it. Ace particularly liked playing hide and seek; he would think he was hidden but you could sometimes see a strange hump of hay moving jerkily across the floor, and often you could see a tail sticking out. Then he would crouch still and suddenly jump out at an older, more stately monkey who was walking by. Gib liked this game as well. There would be a

scramble, then they would both rush away and leap up onto the bars and sit there laughing and chattering.

Almost better than the hay they enjoyed playing on the bars. There were two sets of five bars each, one above the other, reaching right across the cage and fixed to the wall at either end. There were some rope swing bars as well: from the one in the middle they could swoop up onto the top set of bars, or swoop down onto the bottom set. There were three rope swing bars right above the top set near the roof. Ace loved sitting way up there. Also there were three more at the bottom, pretty much in the hay. Here's what they looked like.

They spent hours playing on those bars, rushing about, swinging, jumping, balancing along the top bar, tumbling each other off. Most of the agile monkeys exercised there; one or two who felt too old sat and watched and picked fleas. Ace showed off more than ever.

When they got tired and wanted a rest, both Ace and Gib had favourite places where they liked to be, and they got quite annoyed if other monkeys were in their way. Gibidieff best liked to loll back in a corner over the bottom long bar, then she would stretch up her arms and legs — and tail — and sort of drape herself over the next three bars, so she actually occupied the bottom four bars.

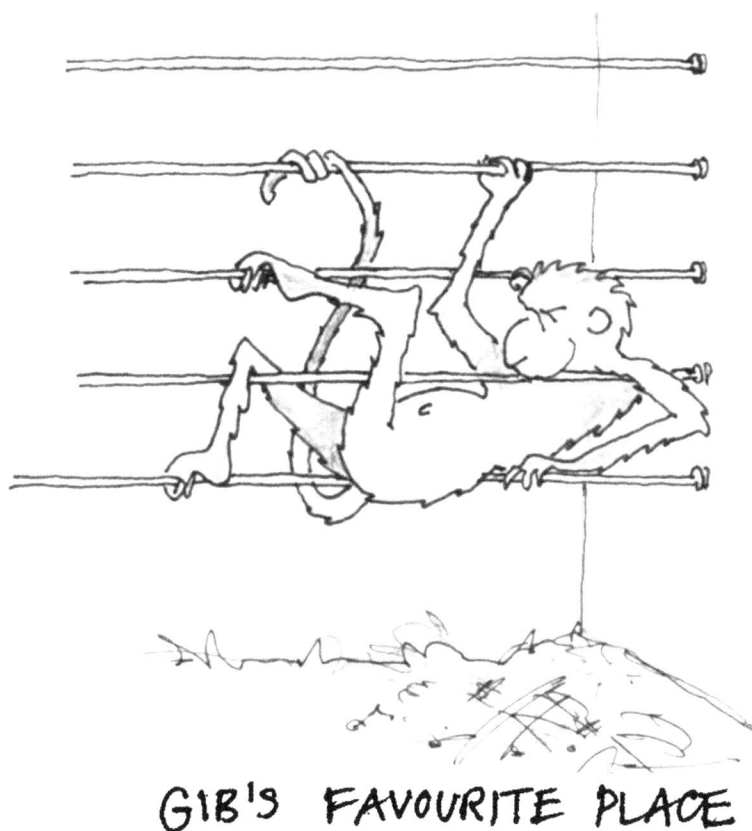

GIB'S FAVOURITE PLACE

But if an older monkey was in that place, she did have another place. She went right up to the top long bar and hung upside-down to rest, stretching across four bars downwards. It looked most peculiar and not very restful at all, but sometimes she stayed still for quite a long time.

GIB'S SECOND FAVOURITE PLACE

ACE'S BEST PLACE

Ace's best place was sitting on the middle swing bar, resting his feet on the top long bar of the bottom set of five and steadying himself by hanging on to the bottom bar of the top set of five. Even if he looked almost asleep his tail used to swish about.

If other monkeys were playing on the middle swing bar, Ace would go right up to the top swing bars or right down on the bottom three bars and hang there relaxing. He found swinging really restful.

There were gaps between the bars. When Gibidieff was in one of her places Ace sometimes sneaked up behind and poked or tickled her through the gaps. They soon found that two could play at that game. When one was resting on the bars the other could creep in behind and be annoying.

One of the keepers specially looked after Ace and Gib. He always knew where they were and what they were doing. He noticed their favourite resting places and thought he would design a set of little labels to fix on the bars so that everyone would know who belonged there.

All the monkeys were keenly interested in the labels. They fingered them and examined them closely and chattered to each other about them. They didn't try to pull them off or spoil them. If you go to that zoo one day you may see them; they might still be there.

Ace and Gib were very proud of them.

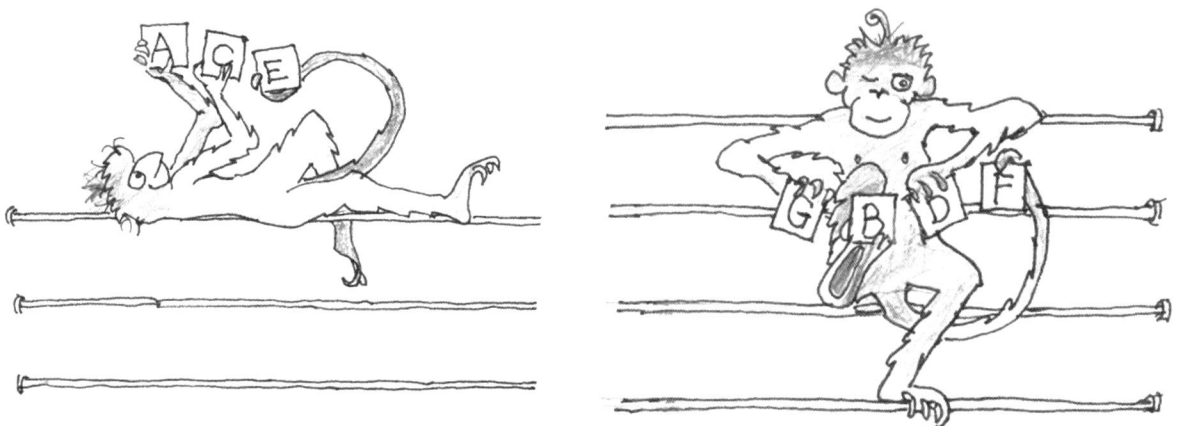

6 STARTER

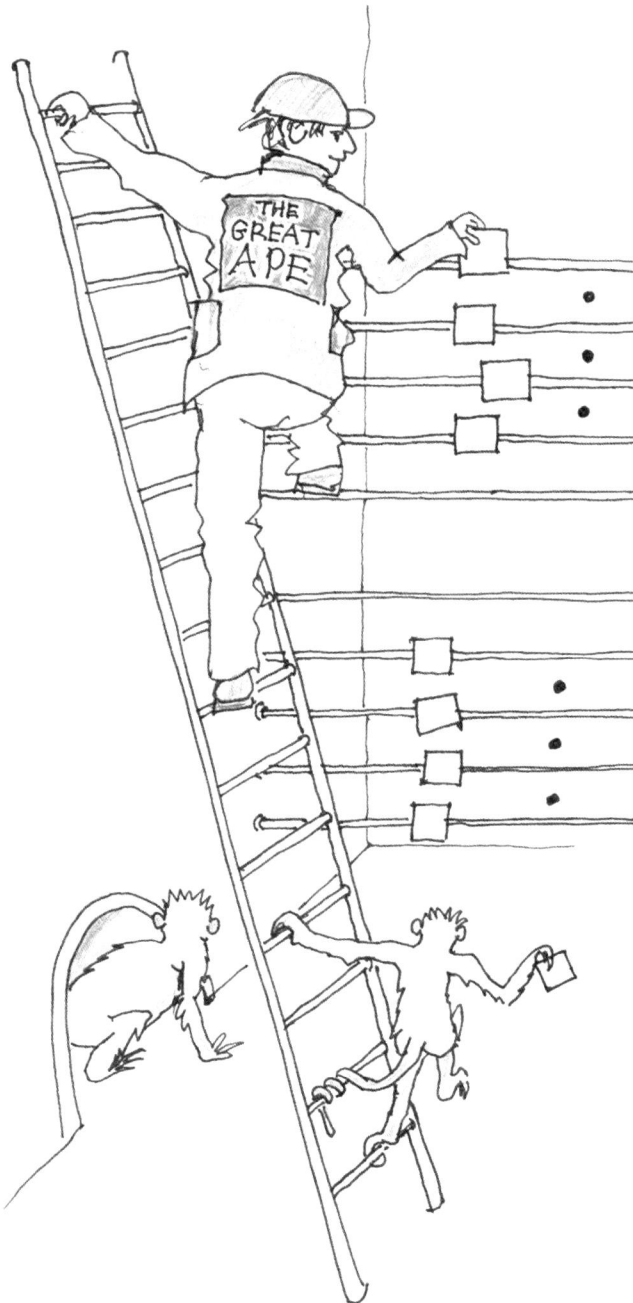

Here are Gibidi-eff's labels   Here are Ace's labels

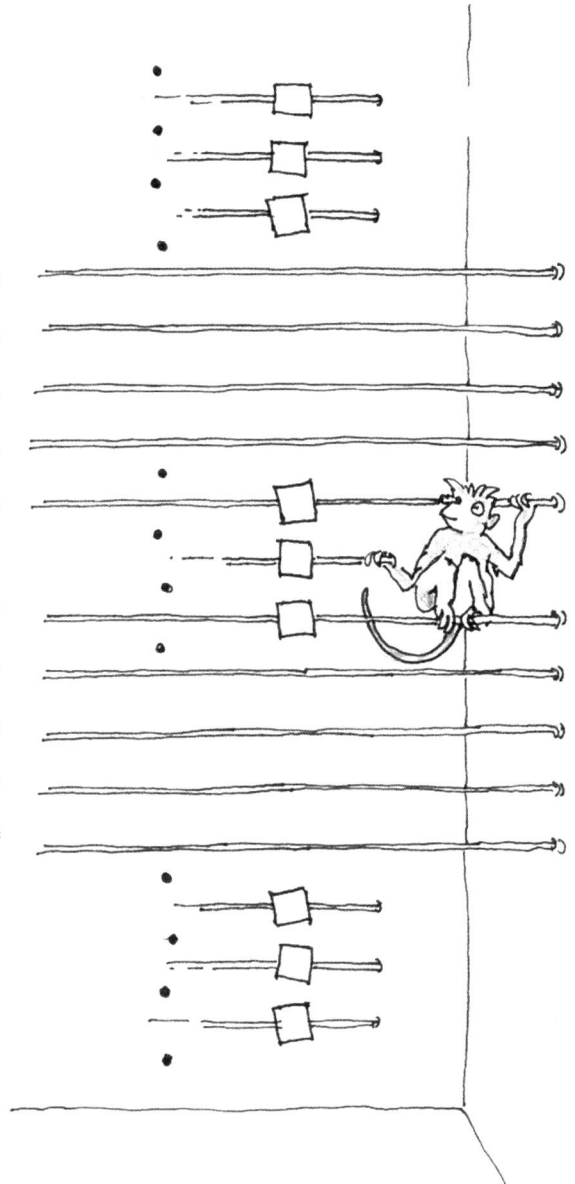

Gibidi-eff's Labels — choose her favourite colour.

- START AT THE BOTTOM, write the letters **G B D F**, one in each label.
- Notice the 3 little dots, they mark the spaces where Ace can get between.
- STARTING AT THE BOTTOM, choose Ace's colour, write **A C E** in the spaces after the dots.

Ace's Lables — use his favourite colour.
- START AT THE BOTTOM and write the letters **A C E**, one in each label.
- Notice the 4 little dots, they mark the spaces where Gibidi-eff can get between.
- STARTING AT THE BOTTOM, use Gib's colour, write **G B D F** in the spaces by the dots.

WRITING NOTES

Music Lines

- In the monkey-house there are two sets of five long bars, and little short bars at the top, middle and bottom for the monkeys to play about on

- Music lines are laid out on exactly the same plan . . . for the music to play about on

- The lines have labels like the keeper made. They are oval and are called **notes**

- They don't have letters written in because people remember where Gib and Ace like to go

- The sets of five long lines are called **staves**

- The sign 𝄞 is called a **treble clef** and shows the higher stave

- The sign 𝄢 is called a **bass clef** and shows the lower stave

- The little line between the two staves is called **middle C**. The correct name for such little lines is **leger lines**

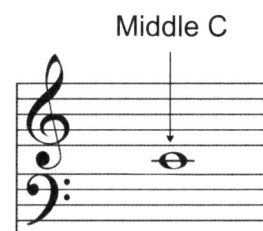

Middle C

GIB'S LINES

You will remember from the story that when she likes to rest Gibidi-eff likes the **bottom four long lines**, also the **top four long lines**, and that she keeps off Ace's two long lines.

So put her letters over or under the dashes. **Start at the bottom**

ACE'S LINES

Also, you will remember that, when resting, Ace keeps off Gib's lines. He likes the places with little lines (leger lines). He likes only two long lines.

Put his letters over or under the dashes. **Start at the bottom**

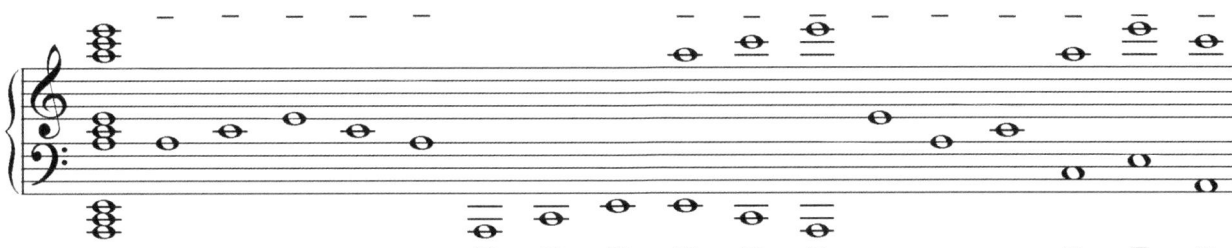

You will have noticed by now:
- that the lines have equal spaces between them (except around middle C where the notes usually need rearranging — see below)

- that there are **three spaces** between Gi-bi-di-eff where Ace can go.

- You will also have noticed that Gibidi-eff needs **four spaces**, and that to get right up or down by Ace's leger lines, Gib needs to use leger lines too, to measure the spaces out.

Put Ace's letters over or under the dashes. Start at the bottom.

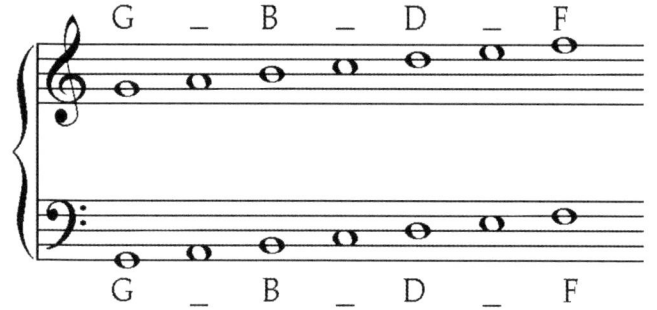

Put Gibidi-eff's letters over or under the dashes. Start at the bottom.

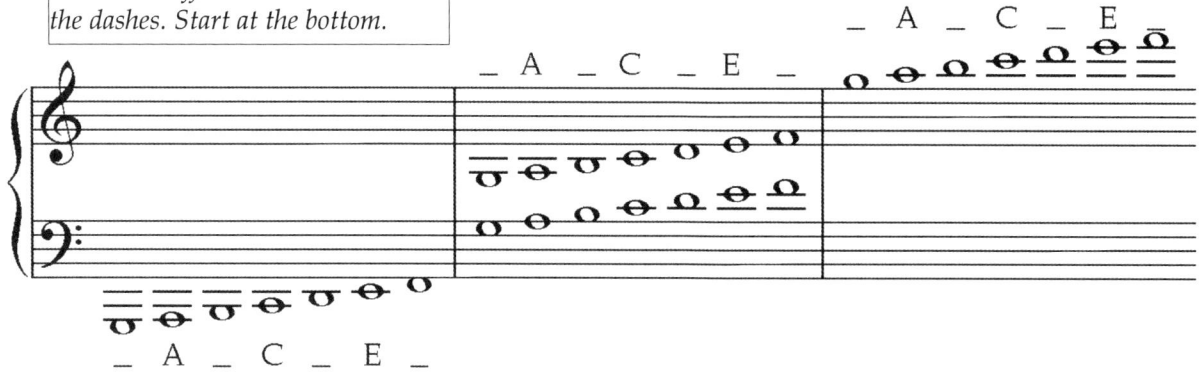

More things to notice:
- that notes next to each other come in alphabetical order
- that G and A come next to each other
- that Gib and Ace between them use all seven letter-names.

Writing Middle C

- In printed music there is quite a big gap between the upper 𝄞 stave and the lower 𝄢 stave.

- When middle C is needed for treble clef music it is printed near the treble clef stave.
- Sometimes the A in Ace's favourite place is also needed for treble clef music, so it is printed on a special leger line underneath middle C

- When middle C is needed for bass clef music it is printed near the bass clef stave.
- Sometimes the E in Ace's favourite place is also needed for bass clef music, so it is printed on a special leger line above middle C

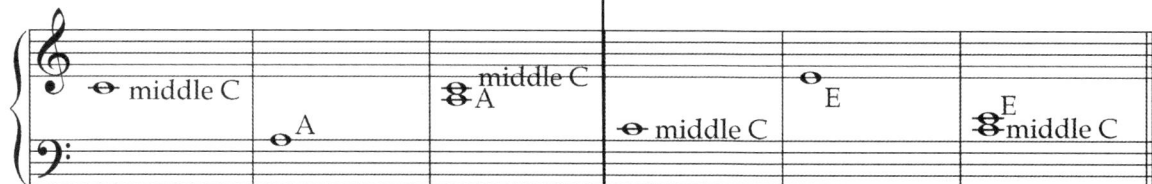

A PUZZLE

- The notes in **Set I** sound exactly the same as the notes in **Set II**. Underline **TRUE** or **FALSE**

- If **TRUE**, how come the notes are in different places although they use the same letter names?

A TEST to be completed from memory

Put the letter names over the dashes.
See if you really know
- which line belongs to whom, and
- who might come through which space

Get someone to mark it, one mark for each correct letter.

SCORES

TOTAL

75-80 Excellent and amazing!   60-74 Pretty good   40-59 OK   Under 40 ? ? ?

Pairs of notes

- Music notes often play in pairs. They can be written above each other, or beside each other
- *2nds are next-door notes*, they have to be written beside each other.

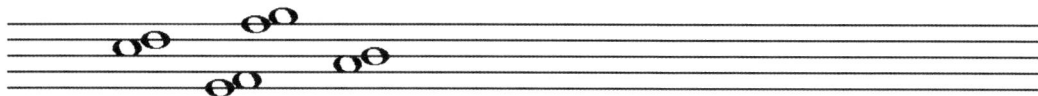

  • You write some . . .

- *3rds are friendly pairs of notes.* If one is on a line, so is the other one; if one moves to a space . . .

  • You write some . . .

- *4ths like to be different:* one on a line, one in a space write some; 4ths, either one above or beside the other.

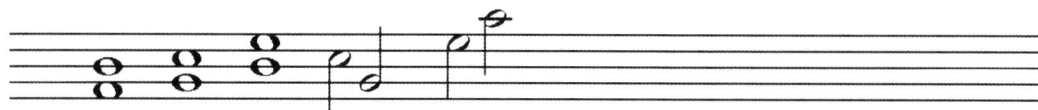

  • You write some . . .

- *5ths always look alike,* both on lines or both in spaces, leaving an empty line or space between for a 3rd to play with them.

  • Write some 5ths

- *6ths are another pair* which often go around together, but they certainly *never look alike* — (might get mistaken for 5ths!)

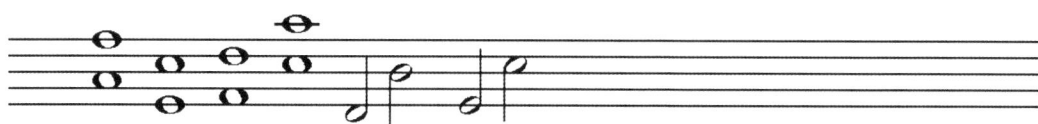

  • Write some 6ths

- *7ths do* look the same, always both on lines or both in spaces, leaving two empty lines or spaces between for 3rds and 5ths.

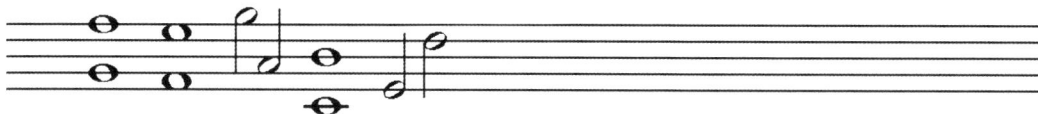

  • Write some 7ths

- Octaves — 8ves — look quite different, but sound very much the same because they have the same letter-names.

- Write some octaves — one on a line, one in a space — it's quite a big gap.

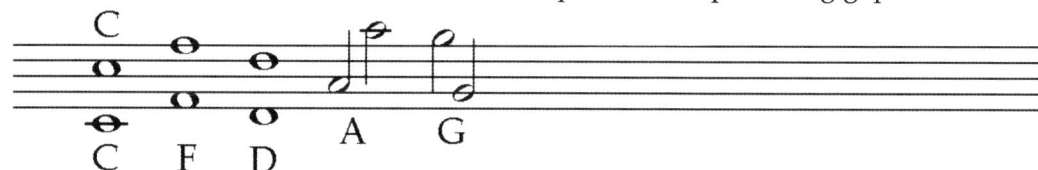

Intervals

- The pairs of notes on the opposite page are called *intervals*
- Intervals are named by their size number – people talk about a 3rd, or a 6th, or an 8ve – meaning a gap between two notes of that particular size
- When you see or hear intervals you can tell them apart
- Here is a line of intervals getting wider as the top line goes up; the bottom note is middle C every time
- Write the correct numbers underneath

- Play these on a piano or keyboard (both hands, any fingers). Middlc C is (you've guessed it!) the C nearest the middle.
- There's more about intervals in section IV; meanwhile, get to recognise how they look and how they sound.

Triads

- Triads are groups of *three notes*
- the notes are written each one above the other
- the interval between the bottom and top notes is a **fifth**
- the other note is the 3rd in the middle
- they can be written using any 5th interval + the 3rd in the middle
- they can be played on a keyboard using thumb, middle and little fingers, either hand, every other note
- The bottom note of a triad is called the **root** of the triad
- Triads are named by the *Root name* eg triad on E, triad on G. Write the root names under the triads
    - There is more to learn about triads in section V. Meanwhile — like the Intervals — get to know them a bit

ROOTS E   _   _   _   G   _

ROOTS E   _   _   _   G   _

Write some 5ths and triads on any notes, or copy the ones above

ROOTS _   _   _   _   _   _

ROOTS _   _   _   _   _   _

Scales

- The word comes from Latin *scala*, and means *a ladder*. One-octave scales are 8 notes long
- on the stave the 8 notes are written *line_space_line_space_ _ _* following each other up (or down). If you start on a line, you will end in a space; if you start in a space . . .
- Practise writing lines of 8 notes here. Use the starting notes
  NOTICE WHICH WAY TO DRAW THE STALKS
  RULE: Notes above the middle line — stalks go *down* on the *left* of the note;
  Notes below the middle line — stalks go *up* on the *right* of the note;
  Notes on the middle line — whichever way looks best.

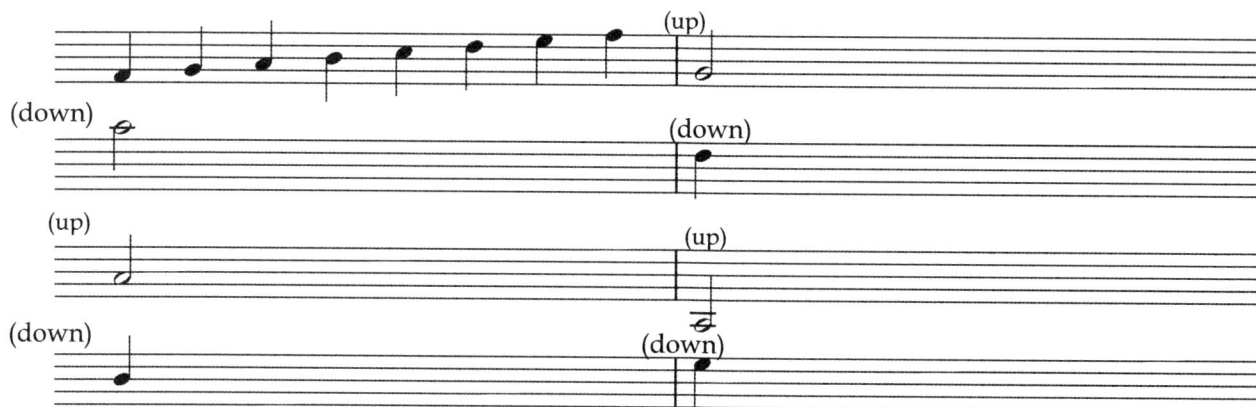

- These staves above have got no clefs. The word *clef* in French means 'a key'; no clefs means no clues to the letter-names.
- When there are clefs and letter-names, you know from your playing
  - each scale starts and finishes with the same letter-name
  - each scale takes its name from the letter-name of the first note
  - each scale needs to use a certain series of sharps, flats and naturals to make it sound major or minor.
- the section called SCALES AND KEYS tells you all you need to know about this; meanwhile practise drawing some ♯s, ♭'s and ♮ 's in the chart below, and in your manuscript book. They need to be very carefully, clearly drawn.

	Vertical	Slanted (parallel)	sharps, flats & naturals on a line	sharps, flats & naturals in a space
Sharps	‖	♯		
Flats	|	(pointed) ♭		
Naturals	‖	(parallel) ♮		

Note Values

From your music study you will have learnt about . . .

- **Beats** – steady pulse-notes throughout a piece of music Conductors beat time for an orchestra or choir.
- **Bars and Barlines** – which divide the pulse-notes into small even groups of 2 or 3 or 4 beats, making the music easier to follow
- **Time signatures** – which show how many pulse-notes are to be in each bar, and what size note the beat-note is to be.

Also you probably know . . .

- that **crotchets** – ♩ – are useful sized beat-notes

- that time signatures **2/4 3/4 4/4** mean 2 crotchets, 3 crotchets, 4 crotchets in each bar

- that if instead of **one crotchet** you see **two quavers** – ♫ – these will take up the same length of time because 2 quavers are worth half a crotchet each.

- that if instead of **two crotchets** you see **one minim** – ♩ – it lasts the same length of time because a minim is worth double a crotchet

- that a **dot beside a note** adds on half the value of the note

- that there are silences (rests) – crotchet rest ⸰ minim rest ▬ quaver rest ⸰ . . .

You probably know lots more . . . .

Music Theory means understanding all these things and learning how to write them properly.

Here are 4 short rhythms using **4/4 3/4 2/4** signatures, crotchets (♩) worth one beat, quavers (♫) worth a ½ beat each, minims (♩) worth 2 beats, (♩·) dotted minims worth 3 beats, (⸰) crotchet rest's worth 1 beat of silence

Rhythm Patterns

- You can study these, work out the sums, and write some different ones which add up correctly. The next section called TIME AND RHYTHM takes you step by step a good long way from here.

Section II
Time and Rhythm

Time Values

- Music notes last for different lengths of time
- Notes (sounds) and rests (silences) have different shapes which show exactly how long they last
- the longest-lasting note (breve) is not often used nowadays

Size	Name	Notes look like	Rests look like
Double semi-breve	Breve	‖O‖	▬
half a breve	Semibreve	O	▬
half a semibreve	Minim	♩	▬
half a minim	crotchet	♩	𝄽
half a crotchet	quaver	♪	𝄾
half a quaver	semiquaver	♬	𝄿
half a semiquaver	demisemiquaver	♬	𝅀

- Note design

hollow notes	largest ‖O‖	next O	next ♩		
black notes	largest ♩	next ♪	next ♪	next ♬	

- Rest design

block rests	largest ▬	next ▬	next ▬		
pattern rests	largest 𝄽	next 𝄾	next 𝄿	next 𝅀	

sometimes in old music 𝄽 is shown by ⸦

BASIC CHART

showing how all the notes fit into a semibreve

One semibreve	**1**	O	which lasts as long as . .
twominims	**2**		which last as long as . .
four crotchets	**4**		which last as long as . .
eight quavers	**8**		which last as long as . .
sixteen semiquavers	**16**		which last as long as . .
thirty-two demi-semiquavers	**32**		

People living in Canada or the United States of America call . . .

semibreves = **whole notes**: minims = **half notes**: crotchets = **quarter notes**: quavers = **eighth-notes**: semiquavers = **sixteenth notes**: demi-semiquavers = **thirty-second notes**

Which do you think is the easiest to remember?

Organising Beats

- Music is for people to join in — singing, playing, whistling,
  even 2-year olds – *"Happy birthday to you"*
- everyone can recognise and join in clapping the **BEAT**or pulse
- crotchets are useful notes to write as beats
- here are twelve crotchets

- organised in groups of 4

- organised in groups of 3

- organised in groups of 2

- these groups are called **BARS**
- In written music you will find
  - BEATS (often crotchets but not always) spaced out by lines | called BAR LINES. When clapping the beats, count how many between the lines — like 1 2 3 4   1 2 3 4   or   1 2 3   1 2 3 or   1 2   1 2. Every time you say 'One' make it louder - an **ACCENT**.

Simple Time Signatures

- These are two numbers printed one above the other on the first stave of the music
- The **top number** tells **how many beats** in each bar
- the **bottom number** shows **which kind of note is the beat note**,
  by using the numbers on the Basic Chart (p. 15) which refer to the different kinds of notes
- crotchet beat — ordinary everyday use - find the number..............................**4**
- minim beat   — slower, more stately music — find the number..................**2**
- quaver beat   — light running or jumping music — find the number **8**

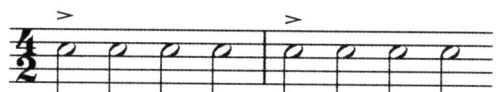

2 How many beats? ____   **3** How many beats? ____   **4** How many beats? ____

4 Beat note name? ____   **8** Beat note name? ____   **2** Beat note name? ____

- give the answers to these, and the three below

- write time signatures which have the following meanings:

- Three crotchet beats

  - Two minim beats

    - Four quaver beats

Do not write time signatures as fractions — no line between

Time Patterns

• Music students quickly learn to play rhythms based on the Basic Chart Time Values
• when learning to write them, start very simply
• be certain the maths is accurate — (they soon get harder)
• Clap this one: *"I like bubble-gum, I like bubble-gum"*

Here's what you were clapping, written in music

can you see how it fits?

• Try another — clap while you say the words

"Our cat's had five lit-tle kit-tens – – –   – – – –"

• and one more — clap as you go

"I don't want an-y-one to help me – – –   – – – – – –"

French time names are an old-fashioned verbal teaching aid to the understanding of rhythms

• 't' sound means the note is struck — *taa*

• 'aa' sound means the note is held — *aa-aa*

• 'ay' sound means the note is halved — *taa-tay*

• 'fy' sound means the note is quartered — *taffy-teffy*

• here's the last pattern with the time-names written over

Taa taa - tay taf - fy tef - fy taa - tay taa taa - tay taf - fy tef - fy taa - tay

• The most useful, using crotchets as beats

clap		say *taa*	one note	— one beat
clap, hold		say *taa-aa*	one note	— two beats
clap, hold, hold		say *taa-aa-aa*	one note	— three beats
clap, hold, hold, hold		say *taa-aa-aa-aa*	one note	— four beats
clap – hold, clap		say *taa-aatay*	two notes	— two beats
• These five patterns use notes smaller than a crotchet		say *taa-tay*	two notes	— one beat
		say *taffy-teffy*	four notes	— one beat
• clap on the beat		say *taa-teffy*	three notes	— one beat
• say the time-names to fit before the next clap		say *taffy-tay*	three notes	— one beat
		say *taa-effy*	two notes	— one beat

18   TIME AND RHYTHM

DOTTED NOTES
- A note or rest can be made *half as long again* by putting a dot beside it

A minim ♩	lasts as long as 2 crotchets ♩♩	A minim with a dot ♩· is a minim and a half	It lasts as long as 3 crotchets ♩ ♩ ♩
A crotchet ♩	lasts as long as 2 quavers ♪♪	A crotchet with a dot ♩· is a crotchet and a half	It lasts as long as 3 quavers ♪♪♪
A quaver ♪	lasts as long as 2 semi-quavers ♬	A quaver with a dot ♪· is a quaver and a half	It lasts as long as 3 semi-quavers ♬♬

- To make ♩· (1½ crotchets) add up to two crotchets you could use ♪ or 𝄾 or ♬

- To make ♪· (¾ crotchet) add up to one crotchet you could use ♪ or 𝄾 or ♬

USING CROTCHETS AS BEAT NOTES —
- make a lively bouncy rhythm by using some dotted notes
- First using even quavers. Say the words and clap a few times

"I've bought my - self   a   love - ly boun-cy ball"

[music: 4/4 rhythm notation]

> Steady, even notes and clapping

- Now change the even quavers ♪♪ — put a dot by the first and a tail on the second ♪·♬

"I've bought my-self   a   love- ly boun - cy ball"

[music: 4/4 rhythm notation]

> Clap this one – very different – it's the dot that does it!

- The dot lengthens the first note, the tail shortens the second
- Here's another

"Beau - ti - ful   sand!   Beau - ti - ful   sea!"

[music: 3/4 rhythm notation]

> Clap the first

- Now lengthen the first crotchet ♩· and shorten the second ♪

"Beau - ti - ful   sand!   Beau - ti - ful   sea!"

[music: 3/4 rhythm notation]

> and the second — see how it works

- this simple method makes these words much more meaningful
- It's very easy — dot by one adds half — tail on the other takes off half
- Hey Presto! • the TIME VALUES of the two notes stay the same
- the RHYTHM PATTERN CHANGES to suit the mood

Note Grouping/Beaming

To make time-patterns easier to read and understand
- beats are planned and grouped into bars: time signatures regulate these
- notes and rests smaller than beats are beamed together to make up blocks worth one beat
— the groups below are worth a crotchet each

- the same applies to dotted patterns — or quaver beats

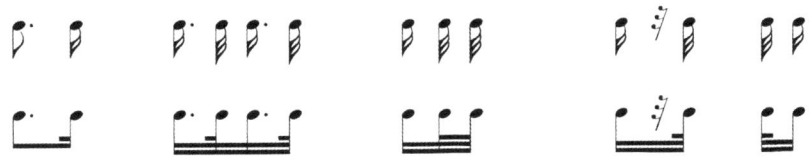

- when studying to find out a time signature
  these blocks will show the size of the beat-notes
- when composing and building a rhythm these blocks form units
  - of the correct size to balance the structure
  - of flexible design to create varied and / or repeated patterns
- rhythm patterns are as characterful and recognisable as tunes —

No prizes!

RULE: Notes are beamed together to form one complete beat
EXCEPTIONS: Other groups of notes which get beamed together:
- in 4 time, if the *first two* or *last two* beats consist of notes smaller than beat notes they
  should if possible be beamed together.

- all four quavers in a bar of $\frac{2}{4}$ time should be beamed together

- bars which consist of all quavers or semiquavers in $\frac{3}{4}$ or $\frac{3}{8}$ time should be beamed together

Compound Time Signatures

Compound means 'made up of two or more parts'
- In compound time *beat notes* are made up of *notes with dots*
- these will divide into groups of three smaller notes

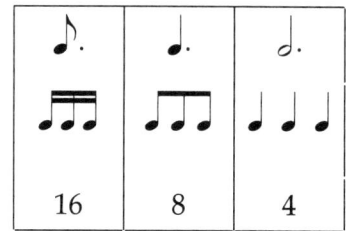

Signature Plan
- Basic Chart (page 15) numbers go at the bottom and show which smaller notes are being used to divide the beat notes. This tells you what the *beat notes* are
- the number of small notes to be found in each bar is shown by the top number, which will always be 6 or 9 or 12
- to find out *how many beats* in each bar, divide the top number by 3

1. *How many beats* in each bar do the following time signatures indicate?

$$\frac{9}{8} \quad \frac{3}{4} \quad \frac{6}{16} \quad \frac{6}{4} \quad \frac{12}{16} \quad \frac{12}{8} \quad \frac{12}{16} \quad \frac{9}{16} \quad \frac{9}{4} \quad \frac{6}{8}$$

2. After each signature write the *3 note group* which makes up each beat

$$\frac{6}{16} \quad \frac{9}{16} \quad \frac{6}{4} \quad \frac{12}{8} \quad \frac{9}{8} \quad \frac{12}{4} \quad \frac{6}{8}$$

3. After each signature write the *dotted beat note* indicated by the signature

$$\frac{6}{4} \quad \frac{12}{8} \quad \frac{12}{16} \quad \frac{9}{4} \quad \frac{9}{8} \quad \frac{12}{4} \quad \frac{6}{16}$$

IN SIMPLE TIME	2 beat signatures	$\frac{2}{4}$ $\frac{2}{2}$		are called *simple duple time*
	3 beat signatures	$\frac{3}{8}$ $\frac{3}{4}$ $\frac{3}{2}$		are called *simple triple time*
	4 beat signatures	$\frac{4}{8}$ $\frac{4}{4}$ $\frac{4}{2}$		are called *simple quadruple time*
IN COMPOUND TIME	2 beat signatures	$\frac{6}{16}$ $\frac{6}{8}$ $\frac{6}{4}$		are called *compound duple time*
	3 beat signatures	$\frac{9}{16}$ $\frac{9}{8}$ $\frac{9}{4}$		are called *compound triple time*
	4 beat signatures	$\frac{12}{16}$ $\frac{12}{8}$ $\frac{12}{4}$		are called *compound quadruple time*

Irregular Time Signatures

$$\frac{5}{8} \quad \frac{7}{8} \quad \frac{5}{4} \quad \frac{7}{4}$$ these are *SIMPLE* time-signatures: the lower number indicates the beat note, the upper number shows how many in each bar

In a short example, a question asking for
- the addition of the time signature, or
- placing of missing bar lines or rests

does not require extra knowledge — just careful counting

Using Rests in Simple and Compound Time

- RULE   A *separate* rest should be used for *each silent beat*

- EXCEPTIONS
    - a *whole bar's rest*. A semibreve rest ▬ is used in *every* time signature
      both simple and compound, except in $\frac{4}{2}$ when a breve rest ▬▬ is used
    - a *half bar's rest*. In quadruple time a single rest is used to fill a half bar's silence
      either at the beginning or at the end of the bar: not in the *middle* of the bar

- In *compound* time a *one beat* rest may be shown either by a dotted rest
  or two rests (first one for the note, then one for the dot)

- In simple or compound time, when completing a bar with rests
    - first, if a *beat* is incomplete finish it with a rest or rests (see ringed beats)
    - next (quadruple time only) if a *half bar* is incomplete finish this (see ②)
    - then finish the bar according to the above rule and exceptions

Musical reasons for using compound time
- The dotted beats used in compound time make it possible to harness the liveliness and fluency
  of many new rhythms available thanks to the triple beat-divisions.
  Unfettered by any 'squareness', these dotted beats can be

- divided evenly into threes, steadily unwinding

  - divided unevenly — two together with one to follow

  - or varied by dots and tails into vigorous movement
    — and many different combinations of these and other patterns

* - one of the rhythms on page 19 should correctly be written in compound time

Section III
Scales and Keys

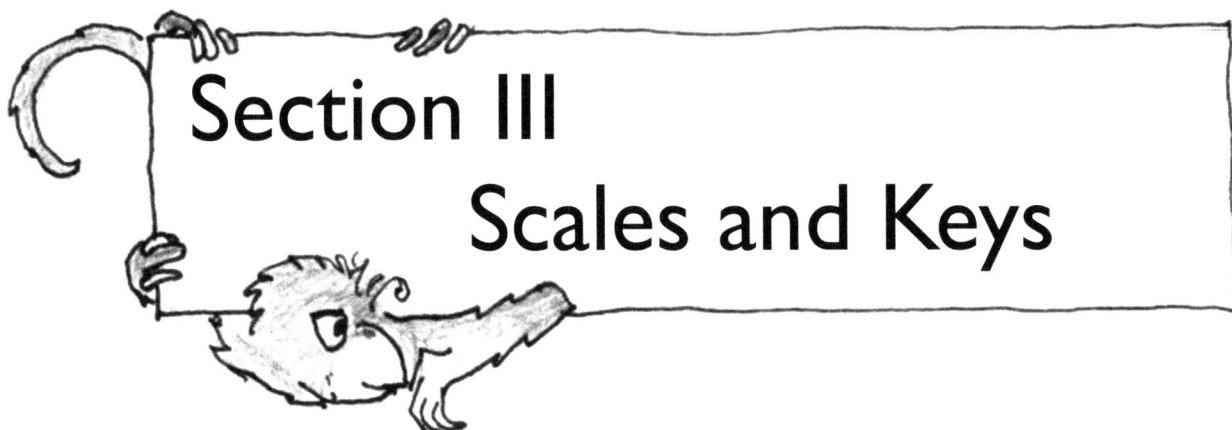

MAJOR SCALES using sharps - how they are constructed

		1	2	3	4	5	6	7	8	*notes going UPWARDS*
Scale of C		C	D	E	F	G	A	B	C	*Use the top 4 notes for the start of*
the scale of G		G	A	B	C	D	E	F♯	G	*Raise the 7th note. Use the top 4 notes for the start of*
the scale of D		D	E	F♯	G	A	B	C♯	D	*Raise the 7th note. Use the top 4 notes for the start of*
the scale of A		A	B	C♯	D	E	F♯	G♯	A	*Raise the 7th note. Use the top 4 notes for the start of*
the scale of E		E	F♯	G♯	A	B	C♯	D♯	E	*Raise the 7th note. . . (there are 3 more sharp keys)*

• semitones are marked

KEY SIGNATURES
The sharps needed for each scale are printed in a neat block next to the clef on each stave.

• copy the 𝄞 and the ♯ signs

MAJOR SCALES using flats - how they are constructed

	8	7	6	5	4	3	2	1	notes going DOWNWARDS
					bottom 4				
Scale of C	C	B	A	G	F	E	D	C	*Use the bottom 4 notes for the start of*
the scale of F	F	E	D	C	B♭	A	G	F	*Lower the 4th note. Use the bottom 4 notes for the start of*
the scale of B♭	B♭	A	G	F	E♭	D	C	B♭	*Lower the 4th note. Use the bottom 4 notes for the start of*
the scale of E♭	E♭	D	C	B♭	A♭	G	F	E♭	*Lower the 4th note. Use the bottom 4 notes for the start of*
the scale of A♭	A♭	G	F	E♭	D♭	C	B♭	A♭	*Lower the 4th note. . . (there are 3 more flat keys)*

• semitones are marked

KEY SIGNATURES
The flats needed for each scale are printed in a neat block next to the clef on each stave.

• *copy the 𝄞 and the ♭ signs*

The three other sharp scales with their key signatures are:

𝔹 F♯C♯G♯D♯A♯   𝔽♯ F♯C♯G♯D♯A♯E♯   ℂ♯ F♯C♯G♯D♯A♯E♯B♯

The three other flat scales with their key signatures are:

𝔻♭ B♭E♭A♭D♭G♭   𝔾♭ B♭E♭A♭D♭G♭C♭   ℂ♭ B♭E♭A♭D♭G♭C♭F♭

MAJOR SCALES   • use 8 next-door letter names
                    • use two different types of 2nds.

        •   minor 2nds or semi-tines   ⌃   two
        •   major 2nds or whole-tones   five

Major scale intervals are arranged thus:

Tone	Tone	Semi-tone	Tone	Tone	Tone	Semi-tone

1 — 2 — 3 — 4 — 5 — 6 — 7 — 8

Tetrachord 1   Tetrachord 2

Each tetrachord (notes 1-4, 5-8) has an identical tonal plan, achieved by
        •raising the 7th in ♯ scales, and
        • lowering the 4th in ♭ scales.

KEY SIGNATURES
        • are the groups of ♯'s or ♭'s printed next to the clef on each stave.
        • they indicate the keynotes which will be realised by their use
        • they apply to all notes of the same letter-name, regardless of pitch
        • an accidental which cancels one of the signature ♯'s or ♭'s
                • only applies to notes of the pitch beside which it is printed
                • only lasts for the bar in which it is printed

• Correct key signatures require exact order and placing

Key notes   G   D   A   E   B   F♯   C♯

Key notes   F   B♭   E♭   A♭   D♭   G♭   C♭

MINOR SCALES

• There are two kinds of minor scale
• both use 8 next-door letter names like major scales
• the different arrangements of major and minor seconds (plus one augmented second) make these two kinds of minor scale sound different from the major and from each other

HARMONIC MINOR SCALES use 3 different types of 2nds
   • minor 2nds or semi-tones ⌒ three
   • major 2nds or whole tones (two semi-tones) three
   • augmented 2nd (three semi-tones) one

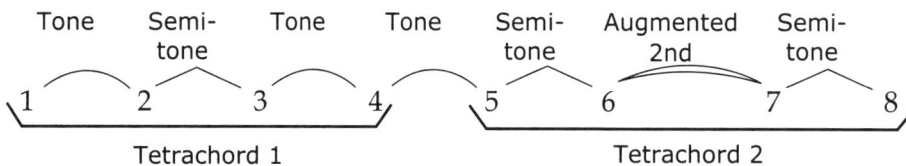

Tone	Semi-tone	Tone	Tone	Semi-tone	Augmented 2nd	Semi-tone
1	2	3	4	5	6 7	8

Tetrachord 1   Tetrachord 2

• The two tetrachords have differing tonal plans
• The augmented 2nd is always between notes 6-7
• The same tonal plan is used both ascending and descending

MELODIC MINOR SCALES use 2 different types of 2nds
   • minor 2nds or semi-tones ⌒ two
   • major 2nds or whole tones five
• the notes used in *tetrachord* 2 vary according to whether the scale is ascending or descending: on the way up the semitone is between notes 7-8; on the way down between notes 6-5

• the intervals are arranged thus

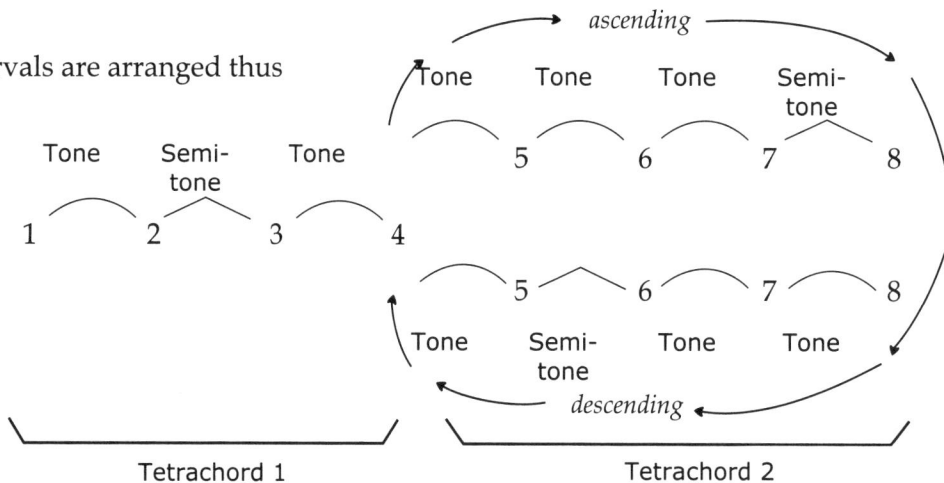

ascending

Tone   Tone   Tone   Semi-tone
   5   6   7   8

Tone   Semi-tone   Tone
1   2   3   4

5   6   7   8
Tone   Semi-tone   Tone   Tone

descending

Tetrachord 1   Tetrachord 2

MINOR KEY SIGNATURES
• a minor key shares a key-signature with its *Relative Major* key
• this close relative is the lowered 3rd note of the tonic major scale, and takes its place as the 3rd note in both minor scales and the minor tonic triad

C major   C minor   E♭ relative major
scale notes and tonic triad   scale notes and tonic triad   key note and signature

• this plan applies to all keys

WRITING SCALES

MAJOR

• Write the clef followed by the signature. Space the notes well

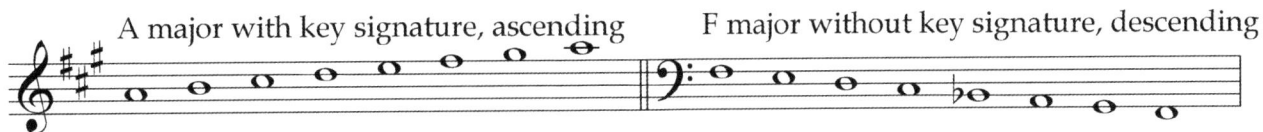

A major with key signature, ascending   *F major without key signature, descending*

• without signature. Write these requirements by the notes they refer to

MINOR

• All minor key signatures act in the same way on tonic major scales. They lower the 3re, 6th and 7th notes
• this is clearly seen below in C minor by using ♭'s: in E minor by removing the #'s

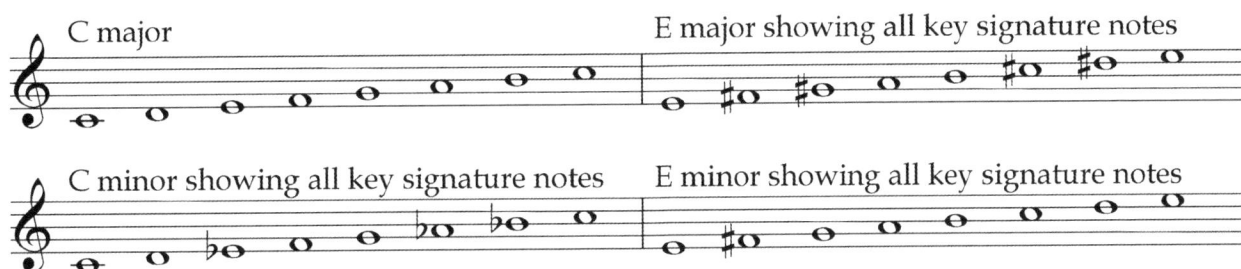

C major   *E major showing all key signature notes*

C minor showing all key signature notes   *E minor showing all key signature notes*

• to write all minor scales   • use the *minor key signature* (*At-a-Glance* page 28)

• to write *harmonic* minors
{
• leave the 3rd alone
• leave the 6th alone
• raise the 7th a semitone
}

• to write *melodic* minors
{
• leave the 3rd alone
• raise the 6th and 7th – going up
• lower them back again * coming down
}

* follow the key signature coming down. It is essential to *check with the key signature* before writing any accidentals

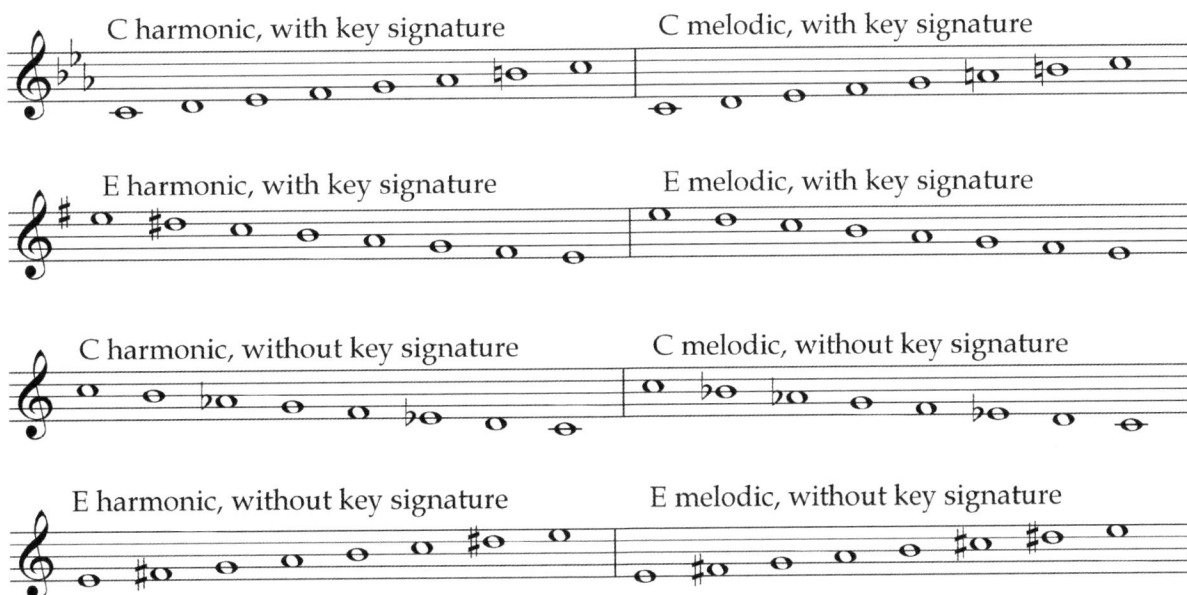

C harmonic, with key signature   *C melodic, with key signature*

E harmonic, with key signature   *E melodic, with key signature*

C harmonic, without key signature   *C melodic, without key signature*

E harmonic, without key signature   *E melodic, without key signature*

The *At-a-Glance* Key Signature Chart

— it's simple to use —

- first study lines ❷ and ❸ carefully left to right
- line ❷ shows numbers down from 7 to 0 and up to 7 again
- line ❸ under the numbers shows the Magic Sentence letters printed twice from left to right with a ◆ under the 0

   — Use lines ❷ and ❸

- to find which ♯'s are needed for a 4♯ signature
  - point to the 4 on the sharp side. Point below
  - D♯ is the 4th sharp. List the four sharps
    starting under the 1, by the ◆ — F♯ C♯ G♯ D♯

- to find which ♭'s are needed for a 3♭ signature
  - point to the 3 on the flat side. Point below
  - A♭ is the 3rd flat. List the three flats
    starting under the 1, by the ◆ — B♭ E♭ A♭

- try one or two more, make sure you understand the system
- using all four lines, look down the columns. *At-a-Glance* is right — you can quickly see any major key note with its signature and relative minor below — or any minor key with the relative major and signature above.
- when listing ♯'s or ♭'s be sure to start by the ◆

← ——— FLAT KEYS   SHARP KEYS ——— →

❶ Major ♭ keynotes	C♭	G♭	D♭	A♭	E♭	B♭	F	C	G	D	A	E	B	F♯	C♯	Major ♯ keynotes	❶
❷ How many ♭'s	7	6	5	4	3	2	1	0	1	2	3	4	5	6	7	How many ♯'s	❷
❸ Key signatures	F♭	C♭	G♭	D♭	A♭	E♭	B♭	◆	F♯	C♯	G♯	D♯	A♯	E♯	B♯	Key signatures	❸
❹ Relative minor keynotes	A♭	E♭	B♭	F	C	G	D	A	E	B	F♯	C♯	G♯	D♯	A♯	Relative minor keynotes	❹

FOUR CATS GO DANCING ALONG EATING BANANAS

magic sentence

IT'S ALSO SIMPLE to draw this chart

- easy and quick to memorise
- very useful to have by you in tests and exams

- Rule the lines - 16 vertical, 5 horizontal
- Outline the 2 middle vertical lines as shown
- Outline the 2 middle horizontal lines as shown

← —————— FLAT KEYS   SHARP KEYS —————— →

❶ Major ♭ keynotes	C							C						C	Major ♯ keynotes ❶
❷ How many ♭'s															How many ♯'s ❷
❸ ?	F							F						A	? ❸
❹ ?	A							A						A	? ❹

- Write FLAT KEYS over the left side, SHARP KEYS over the right side.
 Write numbers **1** to **4** between the lines at each side (as shown)
 On each side by these numbers indicate their meaning.

- Line ❷ Put 0 in the middle, start next to it and write numbers 1-7 in both directions

- Line ❸ – Put ◆ in the middle. Write the magic sentence on each side, starting with F on the left (as shown)

- Line ❶ – starts with **C** for **Cats**. Repeat the magic letters in order using every square. **C** should come first, middle and last (as shown)

- Line ❹ – starts with **A** for **Along**. Repeat the magic letters in order using every square. **A** should come first, middle and last (as shown)

ADD ♭ and ♯ SIGNS

- line ❸ - key signatures: put a sign by every letter − ♭'s on the flat side, ♯'s on the sharp side, starting with F on the left (as shown)

- lines ❶ and ❹ major and minor keynotes − some of these have been made into ♭ or ♯ keynotes by their signatures − These are
 line ❶ major keynotes − put ♭ signs by C G D A E B; put ♯ signs by F C
 line ❹ minor keynotes − put ♭ signs by A E B; put ♯ signs by F C G D A

MEMORISE

- the *Magic Sentence*

- Line ❶ starts with C

- Line ❹ starts with A

PROPER NAMES *for scale notes*

Degrees of scale   • refers to the order of the notes — major or minor
Tonic Sol-fa   • naming major scale notes irrespective of key (esp. vocal use)
Letter Names   • depend on the scale being used (example here C major)
Proper Names   • relate the notes to each other within the key framework — major or minor
Roman Numerals   • used in reference to triads and chords — major or minor

Degrees of scale	1st	2nd	3rd	4th	5th	6th	7th	8th
Tonic sol-fa (major only)	doh	ray	me	fa	soh	la	te	doh
Letter names (example)	C	D	E	F	G	A	B	C
PROPER NAMES	**Tonic**	**Super-tonic**	**Mediant**	**Sub Dominant**	**Dominant**	**Sub Mediant**	**Leading note**	**Tonic**
Roman Numeral	I	II	III	IV	V	VI	VII	I

CHROMATIC NOTES AND SCALES — the word means *many-coloured*

Composers use *chromatic* notes ($\sharp$'s, $\flat$'s, $\natural$'s) extra to the key signature to vary melodies and enrich chords. These notes are called *accidentals*.

CHROMATIC SCALES   • are named by their first letter name
                      • do not have a key-signature
                      • use only minor 2nds (semi-tones)

To write a chromatic scale - one 8ve, 13 notes
• write *one note each* for the 1st, 5th and 8th letter-names (3 notes)
• write *two notes each* for the 2nd, 3rd, 4th, 6th, and 7th letter-names (10 notes)
• plan and fill in the accidentals to sound every semi-tone

Chromatic scale on C

• It is possible to puzzle out accidentals to make all scales accurate
• You will sometimes need to use $\sharp$, $\flat$, $\natural$, $\times$ (double sharp), $\flat\flat$ (double flat)
• you will sometimes need to think of notes by different names (see below)

B	C	E	F					
C$\flat$	B$\sharp$	F$\flat$	E$\sharp$	D$\flat$	E$\flat$	G$\flat$	A$\flat$	B$\flat$
A$\times$	D$\flat\flat$	D$\times$	G$\flat\flat$	C$\sharp$	D$\sharp$	F$\sharp$	G$\sharp$	A$\sharp$

• the various names which can be given to a single sound are called
ENHARMONIC EQUIVALENTS

Section IV
Intervals

an INTERVAL is

- the name given to the different sized gaps between notes
- these have *number-labels* dependent on the letter names used (see Starters) pages 10 & 11
- they also have *type descriptions* dependent on their semi-tone content
- these descriptive words, from the smallest to the largest are

  diminished,   minor,   major,   perfect,   augmented

INTERVALS IN MAJOR KEYS

Type-descriptions of intervals with number labels 2ND, 3RD, 4TH, AND 5TH used in major keys

Type description	Semi-tones	Type description	Semi-tones
minor 2nd	1	perfect 4th	5
major 2nd	2	augmented 4th	6
minor 3rd	3	diminished 5th	6
major 3rd	4	perfect 5th	7

- It is clear from the number of semi-tones how these interval-sizes compare
- on the staves below all possible examples of all these intervals are set out in the key of C major
- they are therefore

ALL WHITE NOTE INTERVALS

- play these (keyboard or piano)
  - study them closely
    - count the semi-tones
      - recognise their shapes
        - listen to them clearly
          - recognise their sounds

MEMORISE THESE WHITE-NOTE INTERVALS

| Major 3rds | | | Minor 2nds | | Augmented 4th | Diminished 5th |
| C to E | F to A | G to B | E to F | B to C | F to B | B to F |

• Repeat these facts

• **C to E, F to A, G to B are *major* thirds**

• **E to F, B to C are *minor* seconds or semi-tones**

• **F to B is an augmented 4th, B to F is a diminished 5th**

Repeat them, parrot fashion, over and over — until you are 100% sure of them. Play them, count the semi-tones, notice that F-B and B-F are the same size interval.

• It is now clear that in terms of white-note intervals all other 2nds are *major*, all other 3rds are *minor*, all other 4ths and 5ths are *perfect*.

TYPE-DESCRIPTIONS OF INTERVALS WITH NUMBER LABELS 6THS, 7THS, AND 8THS USED IN MAJOR KEYS

Type description	Semi-tones
minor 6th	8
major 6th	9
minor 7th	10
major 7th	11
perfect 8ve	12

• again — study them, compare the sizes, notice how they follow on from perfect 5ths in the previous chart.

• Play them and listen to them as they are written out below

• on the stave below examples of all these intervals are set out in the key of C major; again, they are therefore all WHITE NOTE INTERVALS

Minor 6ths			Major 6ths			Major 7th		Minor 7ths				Perfect 8ves			
C	F	G	D	E	A	B	E	B	C	D	F	G	A	C	D	E	F	G
E	A	B	F	G	C	D	F	C	D	E	G	A	B	C	D	E	F	G

34 INTERVALS

Intervals obtainable using ACCIDENTALS
- all intervals can be made smaller or larger by the addition of accidentals. The intervals thus formed add expressive colour and variety of interest to melodies and chords

- 2nds, 3rds, 6ths and 7ths can come in *4 different sizes*

	Type Descriptions	Interval Numbers			
		2nds	3rds	6ths	7ths
Sizes	Diminished	—	2	7	9
	Minor	1	3	8	10
	Major	2	4	9	11
	Augmented	3	5	10	12

Semi-tone count

- 4ths, 5ths, and 8ves can only come in *3 different sizes*

	Type Descriptions	Interval Numbers		
		4ths	5ths	8ves
Sizes	Diminished	4	6	11
	Perfect	5	7	12
	Augmented	6	8	13

Semi-tone count

- in these charts you can find intervals which have the same semi-tone count
- they look different on paper and have different names — but *they sound the same*

Aug 2th	Min 3rd	Maj 6th	Dim 7th	Aug 4th	Dim 5th	Aug 6th	Min 7th
A-B♯	A-C	B-G♯	B-A♭	F-B	E♯-B	F-D♯	F-E♭

RULE: accidentals are always needed when writing augmented or diminished intervals
EXCEPTIONS: the two white note intervals (F-B aug 4th) (B-F dim 5th) memorised, page 32

- for the inquisitive minded. You *can write* a diminished 2nd

it comes out as a unison (single note). It really only exists on paper

D♯ E♭

THE EFFECTS OF ACCIDENTALS ON WHITE NOTE INTERVALS

- columns **1** and **4** display and name different basic white-note intervals
- columns 2 and 3, 5 and 6 display these same white-note intervals with a variety of accidentals which alter the interval sizes and the descriptive names.
- play these through as you study them
- hear how the accidentals alter the sound of each interval

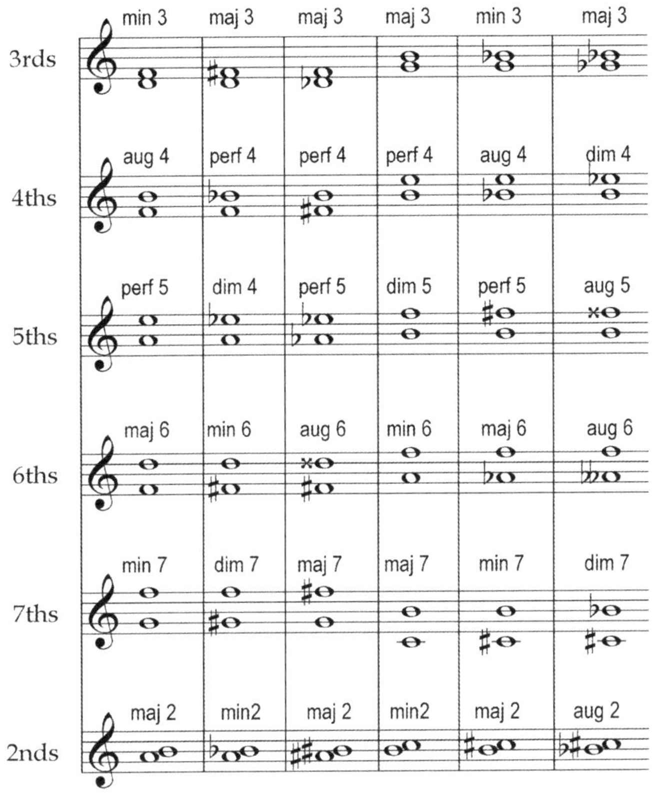

Interval names (left notation table), columns 1–6:

	1	2	3	4	5	6
3rds	min 3	maj 3	maj 3	maj 3	min 3	maj 3
4ths	aug 4	perf 4	perf 4	perf 4	aug 4	dim 4
5ths	perf 5	dim 4	perf 5	dim 5	perf 5	aug 5
6ths	maj 6	min 6	aug 6	min 6	maj 6	aug 6
7ths	min 7	dim 7	maj 7	maj 7	min 7	dim 7
2nds	maj 2	min2	maj 2	min2	maj 2	aug 2

Description table, columns 1–6:

	1	2	3	4	5	6
3rds	minor 3rd	top note↑ interval bigger	bottom note↓ interval bigger	maj 3rd	top note↓ interval smaller	both notes↓ no change
4ths	aug 4th	top note↓ interval smaller	bottom note↑ interval smaller	perf 4th	bottom note↓ interval bigger	top note↓ interval smaller
5ths	perf 5th	top note↓ interval smaller	both notes↓ no change	dim 5th	top note↑ interval bigger	top note↑↑ interval bigger
6ths	maj 6th	bottom note↑ interval smaller	top note↑↑ bottom↑ interval bigger	min 6th	bottom note↓ interval bigger	bottom note↓↓ interval bigger
7ths	min 7th	bottom note↑ interval smaller	top note↑ interval bigger	maj 7th	bottom note↑ interval smaller	top note↓ bottom↑ interval smaller
2nds	maj 2nd	top note↓ interval smaller	both notes↑ no change	min 2nd	top note↑ interval bigger	top note↑ bottom↓ interval bigger

EXPERIMENT: Method: Invert some 6ths and 7ths, put the top notes to the bottom. Play them

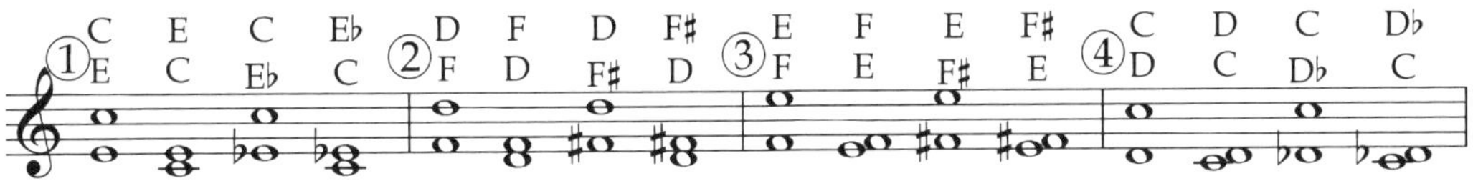

① C/E E/C C/E♭ E♭/C ② D/F F/D D/F♯ F♯/D ③ E/F F/E E/F♯ F♯/E ④ C/D D/C C/D♭ D♭/C

Conclusion: this experiment shows that

- when a *minor 6th* is inverted it becomes a *major 3rd*
- when a *major 6th* is inverted it becomes a *minor 3rd*
- when a *major 7th* is inverted it becomes a *minor 2nd* (semi-tone)
- when a *minor 7th* is inverted it becomes a *major 2nd* (tone)

Play them till you can hear that this conclusion is correct

- the above conclusion helps with identifying 6ths and 7ths;
- their inversions (3rds and 2nds) have been memorised
- they are simpler to identify than larger intervals
- perfect 4ths when inverted become perfect 5ths, and vice versa

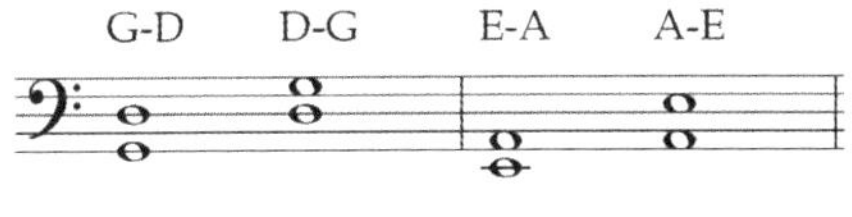

G-D   D-G   E-A   A-E

KEY-RELATED WORK

• THE RELATION BETWEEN proper names AND SCALE LETTER NAMES is demonstrated on these two pages by two charts using a selection of major and minor keys

CHART 1   MAJOR SCALES

• all degrees, proper names, tonics and numbers of ♯'s and ♭'s are printed
• some letter-names and key signature requirements are printed
  Starting from the lower tonic, YOU write in
    • the missing letter-names in keys B F♯ E♭ A♭ D♭
    • the key signature requirements — (At-a-Glance chart page 28)

Degrees of scale	PROPER NAMES	MAJOR SCALES								
8th	TONIC	C	D	A			F			
7th	LEADING NOTE	B	C♯	G♯			E			
6th	Sub-mediant	A	B	F♯			D			
5th	DOMINANT	G	A	E			C			
4th	SUB-DOMINANT	F	G	D			B♭			
3rd	Mediant	E	F♯	C♯			A			
2nd	Supertonic	D	E	B			G			
1st	TONIC	C	D	A	B	F♯	F	E♭	A♭	D♭
KEY SIGNATURE REQUIREMENTS ⟶		–	2♯'s	3♯'s	5♯'s	6♯'s	1♭	3♭'s	4♭'s	5♭'s

Identifying intervals in major keys

• Questions may give intervals and ask for any one major key in which each can be found

    • if the interval is a perfect 4th or 5th either note can be the tonic
    • if the interval is neither of these two, the sharpest note can be the leading note (7th)
    • if both notes are white the key can always be C major

• Questions may give 2 or 3 intervals and ask for a major key where _all_ can be found.

    • list the accidentals: the sharpest (leading note) gives the key note
    • if all flats and naturals, check with _At-a-Glance_ chart for signature

• keep your _White Note Interval memory work_ to the fore

CHART 2   HARMONIC MINOR SCALES

When working on the *Harmonic Minor* chart, proceed exactly as above. Also
- raise the 7th degree of each scale (leading note) by a semitone
- to achieve this put the accidental into the little ☐
- if the key signature does not affect the 7th, put a ♯
- if the key signature has flattened the 7th, cross out the ♭ and put a ♮
- if the key signature has sharpened the 7th, cross out the ♯ and put a ✕ (double sharp)

Degrees of scale	PROPER NAMES	HARMONIC MINOR SCALES							
8th	TONIC	A	E		F		C♯		
7th	LEADING NOTE	[♯] G	[♯] D	[ ]	[♮] E✕	[ ]	[♯] B	[ ]	[ ]
6th	Sub-mediant	F	C		D♭		A		
5th	DOMINANT	E	B		C		G♯		
4th	SUB-DOMINANT	D	A		B♭		F♯		
3rd	Mediant	C	G		A♭		E		
2nd	Supertonic	B	F♯		G		D♯		
1st	TONIC	A	E	G	F	B♭	C♯	G♯	C
KEY SIGNATURE REQUIREMENTS ⟶		–	1♯	2♭'s	4♭'s	5♭'s	4♯'s	5♯'s	3♭'s

Identifying intervals in minor keys (as in major keys, page 36)

- if intervals dim 4th, aug 5th, aug 2nd, dim 7th are formed because of the absence of key signature, the *leading note* may have no accidental:

  It is always one of the notes in these intervals (only found in minor keys)

- mixed accidentals ♯/♭, ♭/♮ : the sharpest is leading note in a minor key

Become familiar with Proper Names in Interval Work
- all 5ths in major keys are perfect except *Leading note - sub dominant*
- all 4ths in major keys are perfect except *sub dominant - leading note*
- in major keys semi-tones occur between *mediant - sub dominant,* and *leading note - tonic*
- in minor keys keys the signature always gives *minor intervals* up from the *tonic* to the *mediant* (3rd), *sub-mediant* (6th), *leading note* (7th)
- in minor keys major thirds come between *mediant - dominant, sub mediant - tonic* and *dominant - leading note* (if it has been raised)
- play these intervals in different keys — tell yourself these facts — think in terms of proper names

- In all minor keys
  - the key signatures always lower the 3rd, 6th and 7th of the tonic major key
  - never affect the 2nd, 4th or 5th of the tonic major key

- the scales printed below show clearly how
  - the presence of flats in the signature affects the 3rd, 6th and 7th in key C minor
  - the absence of sharps in the signature affects the 3rd, 6th and 7th in key E minor

Notes of C major   Notes of C minor

Notes of E major   Notes of E minor

- the intervals printed below show the differences and similarities between the major and the minor modes

| Maj 2 | Maj 3 | Perf 4 | Perf 5 | Maj 6 | Maj 7 | | Maj 2 | Min 3 | Perf 4 | Perf 5 | Min 6 | Min 7 |

| — | Maj 3 | — | — | Maj 6 | Maj 7 | | — | Min 3 | — | — | Min 6 | Min 7 |

- in all minor keys the intervals from the tonic correspond to the above
- in all minor keys an accidental is needed to sound a semitone between 7th and 8th degree

FOUR NEW INTERVALS

- the *raising of the leading note* (7th) in minor keys and scales combines with the minor signature to introduce four new intervals, intensely valuable in establishing the character of the minor mode

- ① 3rd – 7th aug 5th   E♭–B♮   Aug 5

- ② 7th – 3rd dim 4th   B♮–E♭   Dim 4

- ③ 6th – 7th aug 2nd   A♭–B♮   Aug 2

- ④ 7th – 6th dim 7th   B♮–A♭   Dim 7

- It will be noticed that
  - intervals ① and ② are the same notes inverted, as are ③ and ④; this bears out the conclusions regarding inverted intervals, page 35
  - without raising the *leading note* by the use of an accidental (in this key B♮) none of these intervals would be obtainable

QUESTIONS – methods and working notes

Questions on intervals fall into two types [see **Question Section**]

Type 1 – Intervals unrelated to keys. Some typical questions

- given an interval. State full name (number and description)

- given the description of an interval. Write an example of one.

- given the description and one of the notes. Write the other note

- given an interval. Name it, invert it, name the inversion

- given an interval. Name it; make it larger or smaller by adding or removing an accidental. Name the new interval.

Type 1   If you do not immediately recognise the interval, either
- count the letter-names, then the semi-tones, or
- remove any printed accidental(s)
- name the resulting white-note interval,
- replace the accidental(s) and decide how it / they affect the white-note interval

Type 2 – Intervals related to keys. Some typical questions

Question ①   fully describe this interval   Name 2 major keys which contain it.
The interval is a minor 6th. The major keys which contain it
- must have E♭, must not have G♭ in their key signatures
At-a-Glance chart page 28
- on the chart MAJOR KEYS C♭   G♭   D♭   A♭   E♭   B♭   F
SIGNATURES F♭   C♭   G♭   D♭   A♭   E♭   B♭

- you can see – keys which have E♭ but not G♭ are B♭   E♭   A♭

Question ② Name this interval . . . .   Name a key in which it occurs. . . . .

[working notes. White notes F-E, major 7th   } mixed accidentals means
with top lowered and bottom raised <u>Diminished</u> 7th   } *minor* key
sharpest note F#, leading note for G

Ans. **Dim 7th;   G minor**]

Question ③ Name this interval . . . .   Name *two* keys in which it occurs. . . . .

[working notes: an easy one   } either note could be the tonic
perfect 5th   }

Ans: **perfect 5th;   A♭, E♭ major**

40 INTERVALS

WORKING NOTES

(answers in **shaded boxes)**

Question ④

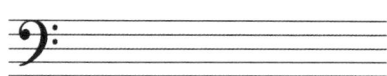

𝄢 ═══════════════ write the key signature for B minor, followed by a major 3rd and a
minor 7th in that key

[working notes. *At-a-Glance* chart on page 28, signature of 2♯'s.

Major 3rd in a minor key is mediant-dominant: in B min is D-F♯

Major 2nd is tonic-supertonic, inverted supertonic-tonic, minor 7th. In B minor C♯-B

Answer: **key signature F♯ C♯; major 3rd D-F♯; minor 7th C♯-B**]

Question ⑤

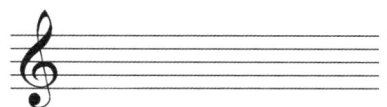

𝄞 ═══════════════ Using the notes of F minor write the following intervals:
dim 4th, minor 6th, minor 10th. Do not use a key signature

[working notes. *At-a-Glance* for key signature B♭ E♭ A♭ D♭

Dim 4th is Leading note-mediant E-A♭ (write ♭'s by the intervals)

Min 6th is Tonic-sub med F-D♭ (minor key sig always lowers 6th)

Min 10th is same as min 3rd F-A♭ (see below: Compound Intervals)

Answer: **Dim 4th E-A♭; min 6th F-D♭; min 10th F-A♭**]

list proper names with scale notes, also raise leading note	
Tonic	F
L note	E♮ ♮
Sub med	D♭
Dominant	C
Sub dom	B♭
Mediant	A♭
Supertonic	G
Tonic	F

Question ⑥

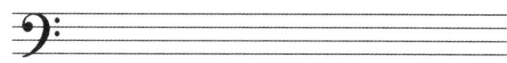

𝄢 ═══════════════ write the key signature of 5
sharps and name the minor key
which uses it. In this key write intervals of a perfect 4th, and an augmented
2nd. Invert these and rename them

[working notes. *At-a-Glance* for key sig **F♯ C♯ G♯ D♯ A♯ - G♯ minor**

Perf 4th: tonic-sub dom **G♯-C♯** *inverted is* **Perfect 5th C♯-G♯**

Aug 2nd is always sub med-lead note **E-F𝄪** inverted is **dim 7th F𝄪-E**]

List proper names with notes: raise leading note (double ♯)	
Tonic	G♯
L note	F𝄪 ×
Sub med	E
Dominant	D♯
Sub dom	C♯
Mediant	B
Supertonic	A♯
Tonic	G♯

COMPOUND INTERVALS

• are intervals greater than an 8ve

• are described as the simple intervals shown

• are numbered as the simple interval shown
 plus 7

maj 2nd	maj 9th	maj 3rd	maj 10th	perf 4th	perf 11th	perf 5th	perf 12th
min 2nd	min 9th	min 3rd	min 10th	aug 4th	aug 11th	dim 5th	dim 12th

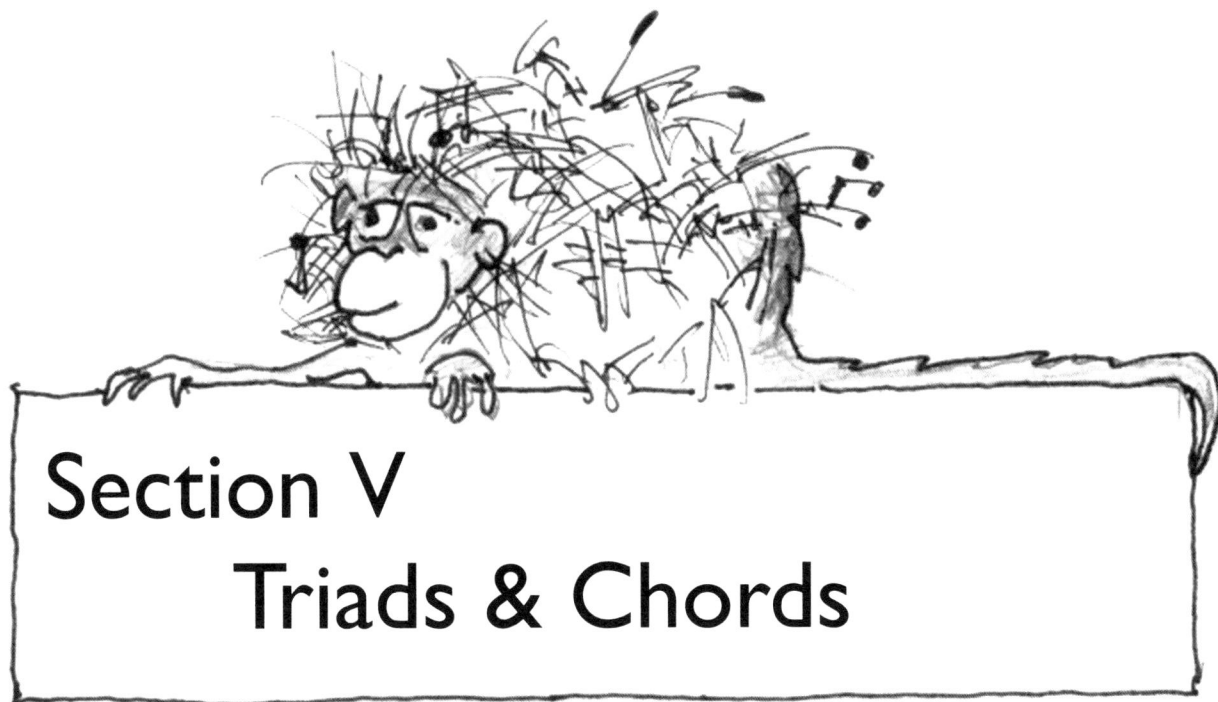

Section V
Triads & Chords

TRIADS AND CHORDS

- Triads are 3-note chords.   They are equally spaced with one letter-name between each note:

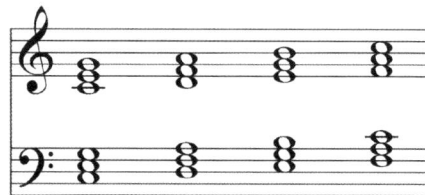

C d E f G   D e F g A   E f G a B

- Five fingers placed over 5 next-door white notes on a keyboard will cover a triad played by thumb, middle and little fingers.
- The bottom note is called the **ROOT**,
  the middle note is called the **THIRD**,
  the top note is called the **FIFTH**

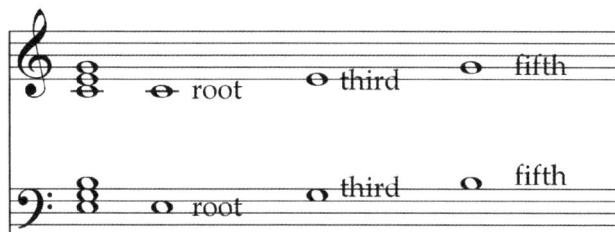

- Triads do not all sound exactly the same.

- Work with *Triads* relates closely to work with *Intervals* – section IV

THE DIFFERENCE IN SOUND between MAJOR and MINOR triads
- Both major and minor triads consist of the same *outside interval – a perfect 5th* divided by a middle note into *2 intervals of a 3rd each*, one on top of the other
  - The *larger* 3rd   (4 semitones) is a *major 3rd*
  - The *smaller* 3rd (3 semitones) is a *minor 3rd*

    - a triad which has.................the *larger* (major) 3rd below
                          and the *smaller* (minor) 3rd above it
      sounds MAJOR and is called a *MAJOR TRIAD*

    - a triad which has.................the *smaller* (minor) 3rd below
                          and the *larger* (major) 3rd above it
      sounds MINOR and is called a *MINOR TRIAD*

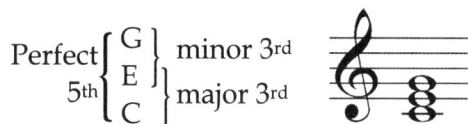

MAJOR TRIAD

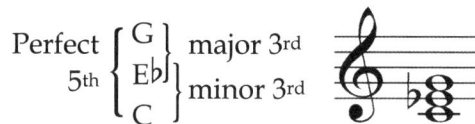

MINOR TRIAD

- on a keyboard it's very easy to change triads from major into minor and back

- try it; raise or lower the 3rd

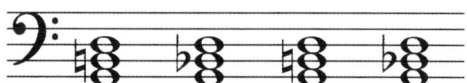

- decide by the sound which is major and which is minor

- Triads are used in all keys, both major and minor.
- Every degree of the scale is the *root* (bottom note) of its own triad: *which kind of triad* it is depends on the layout of the semitones
-        next; two other triads – AUGMENTED and DIMINISHED triads

Name	Consists of	Overall number of semitones	Outside interval`
Augmented triad	2 major 3rds	8	Augmented 5th
Diminished triad	2 minor 3rds	6	Diminished 5th

AUGMENTED triad
two major thirds

$$\text{Aug 5th} \begin{cases} \text{G}^\sharp \\ \text{E} \\ \text{C} \end{cases} \begin{matrix} \text{major 3rd} \\ \text{major 3rd} \end{matrix}$$

DIMINISHED triad
two minor thirds

$$\text{Dim 5th} \begin{cases} \text{G}^\flat \\ \text{E}^\flat \\ \text{C} \end{cases} \begin{matrix} \text{minor 3rd} \\ \text{minor 3rd} \end{matrix}$$

These two are both easily recognisable, strange-sounding triads.

- Whether you are a keyboard player or not, get used to the look, the feel, and above all *the sound* of the different triads
- Work out and play some different triads on a piano
- Use any keys you are familiar with
- Decide by the sound how each one should be described
- Then check by counting semitones

TRIADS IN MAJOR KEYS

The order of triads in MAJOR KEYS

Note names	Tonic	Super-tonic	Mediant	Sub-dominant	Dominant	Sub-mediant	Leading note
Roman numeral	I	II	—	IV	V	—	—
Degrees	1st	2nd	3rd	4th	5th	6th	7th
Triad order	major	minor	minor	major	major	minor	diminished

- Mediant, sub-mediant, leading note triads get to be studied in later grades
- ROMAN NUMERALS **I IV** and **V** mark *Tonic, Subdominant and Dominant Triads* — called *Primary triads*
- in a MAJOR KEY these PRIMARY triads sound MAJOR

- NUMERAL **II** marks *Super-tonic Triad* — called a *Secondary triad*
- in a MAJOR KEY this SECONDARY triad sounds MINOR

Some examples of TRIADS I II IV V in different *major keys*. Copy the clefs, key signatures and triads. Write the key-note names.

- Helpful — jot in rough note names for each scale and ♯'s or ♭'s needed
- Use the *At -a-Glance* chart to check signatures and key notes (page 28)

Ex. A   Copy

I II IV V   I II IV V

Keynote_____

Ex. B   Copy

I II IV V   I II IV V

Keynote_____

Ex. C   Copy

I II IV V   I II IV V

Keynote_____

Ex. D   Copy

I II IV V   I II IV V

Keynote_____

- As shown in Ex. A below, write the letter-names of the triads you have completed in Ex. B, C and D above. Remember to name sharp or flat notes as required by the key signature

Chords	Ex. A	Ex. B	Ex. C	Ex. D
I	G B D			
II	A C E			
IV	C E G			
V	D F♯ A			

TRIADS IN MINOR KEYS

• The order of triads in MINOR KEYS

Note names	Tonic	Super-tonic	Mediant	Sub-dominant	Dominant	Sub-mediant	Leading note
Roman numeral	I	II	–	IV	V	–	–
Degrees	1st	2nd	3rd	4th	5th	6th	7th
Triad order	minor	diminished	augmented	minor	major	major	diminished

• ROMAN NUMERALS **I IV** and **V** mark *Tonic, Subdominant and Dominant Triads* — called *Primary triads*

* Triad **V** (Dominant triad)
• the middle note of triad V is the 7th degree of the scale and the leading note of the key.
• *minor key signatures* never raise leading notes; an *accidental* is always needed to form the semitone between the leading note and the note above it.
• in minor keys dominant triads will *always* need an accidental in front of the 3rd – middle note.

• in a MINOR KEY these PRIMARY triads sound **I** minor, **IV** minor, ***V** major
• Roman numeral **II** marks the *Supertonic Triad* — called a *Secondary triad*
• in a minor key this secondary triad sound *diminished*

HERE ARE Minor key signatures, Minor tonic triads, Dominant triads

Question "In each example, add the necessary accidental to the dominant triad which will raise the leading note to form a semitone below the tonic. Name the key."

• middle note (third) of the *Dominant triad* needs raising
• check the effect of the key signature upon this middle note, which is the the leading note (7th) of each different key
• if the key signature puts a ♭, you put a ♮
• if the key signature puts a ♮, you put a ♯
• if the key signature puts a ♯, you put a ✕ (double sharp)

TRIAD INVERSIONS
TRIAD INVERSIONS in close position

- Up to now all triads have been written with their ROOTS IN THE *BASS — *(lowest sounding). With this arrangement the triad is said to be in ROOT POSITION

- If the THIRD IS IN THE BASS with the fifth in the middle and the root at the top, the triad is called a FIRST INVERSION

- If the FIFTH IS IN THE BASS with the root in the middle and the third at the top, the triad is called a SECOND INVERSION

- they obviously sound different. On paper their shapes are different

EXAMPLE
- *Four different triads*   C major,   E major,   E♭ major   A minor
  Notes (root position order)   C E G   E G♯ B   E♭ G B♭   A C E
  The inversions use the same notes, different order

It is clear from studying the triads in this example
- in *Root Position* both intervals are 3rds
- in *1st Inversion* the lower interval is a 3rd, the upper one is a Perfect 4th (shaded black)
- in *2nd Inversion* the lower interval is a Perfect 4th, the upper one is a 3rd
- whether the 3rds are major or minor depends upon the key

Play the following triads. Name the triads (major or minor) and state the position, as e.g. ①

Triad *D maj* Position   Triad . . . . . Position   Triad . . . . . Position   Triad . . . . . Position
       Root

Triad . . . . . Position   Triad . . . . . Position   Triad . . . . . Position   Triad . . . . . Position

- to name the triads *find the root* — 1st inversion: it's at the **top**; 2nd inversion: it's in the **middle**

INVERSIONS continued

There are two ways of indicating which triad position is intended to be used above a given bass note

1. By Roman Numerals and lower case letters: e.g. triads in key D major

I Ib Ic II IIb IIc IV IVb IVc V Vb Vc

2. By numbers written below the bass notes, indicating the intervals to be used to form the chords above them. Bass notes will not have numbers if

- the bass note is to be the root of the chord
- the bass note is a passing note not suggesting a change of harmony

Tonic   Supertonic   Subdominant   Dominant

| 6 | 6 | 6 | 6 | 6 | 6 | 6 | 6 |
| (3) | 4 | (3) | 4 | (3) | 4 | (3) | 4 |

- This is a very economical way of indicating triads (or chords): guitarists and jazz players get very used to following numbered music

- no figures always means use a ROOT POSITION

FIRST INVERSION
- a 6 chord is another name for a first inversion
- the number (3) under the 6 in a 1st inversion is assumed and often omitted

The note required is D, the middle note will be A (the third is always taken for granted). This will form the first inversion of the triad / chord of D

SECOND INVERSION
- a $\frac{6}{4}$ chord is another name for a second inversion

- $\frac{6}{4}$ chords are an important part of cadential progressions (see page 51)

- count the gaps upwards *including* the bass note

the notes required are B and G and will form the second inversion of the triad / chord of G

CHORDS

CHORDS are triads extended and spread out to suit the requirements of the music: the three basic notes can be repeated at a different pitch or by different instruments or voices: extra notes can be added to the chords, passing notes can be used between them: there is no limit. In the early stages the study of chords follows the same pattern as the study of triads.

Below and opposite are two passages and questions about them, followed by a careful method for arriving at the answers.

A
1. 2. 3.   4. 5. 6.

Question 1 Name the major key of the passage A and identify the triads used by means of Roman numerals written below them.

Where the triads are not in root position, indicate this by the use of letters b or c beside the Roman numerals

METHOD — What to do — see below for how to do it

- Draw the diagram in your manuscript book
- Find keynote of passage A. *At-a-Glance* p. 28: **B♭ major** Passage B is given, **G major**
- In column ① write the Proper Names starting at the bottom. Go up 9 places
- In column ② write Roman Numerals in the correct places
- In columns ③ and ④ write the scale letter-names of B♭ and G major plus key signature #'s or ♭'s
- In columns ⑤ and ⑥ write the triad letter-names for the 4 triads in both keys. If in doubt refer to the diagram on page 45
- ⑦ list the letter-names used in triads 1-6 in passage A. Match them with triad notes in column ⑤. Decide which triad, which position. Answer the question using numerals and lower case letters.

⑦ Triads in Passage A
1 G C E♭ – IIc
2 F A C – V
3 F B♭ D – Ic
4 G B♭ E♭ – IVb
5 F A C – V
6 D F B♭ – Ib

Here's how to do it . . .

		Key notes				Triad notes	
		Key B♭	Key G			Key B♭	Key G
	supertonic	C	A				
	tonic	B♭	G				
	leading note	A	F#				
	submediant	G	E				
V	dominant	F	D	V		F A C	D F# A
IV	subdominant	E♭	C	IV		E♭ G B♭	C E G
	mediant	D	B				
II	supertonic	C	A	II		C E♭ G	A C E
I	tonic	B♭	G	I		B♭ D F	G B D
②	①	③	④			⑤	⑥

Question 2. Identify the chords used in Passage B (key G major) by writing Roman numerals in the brackets printed below the stave. In bars 3 and 4 indicate the chord positions by the use of letters b or c beside the numerals. Disregard any extra or passing notes

"Bend the sapling"

METHOD Numbers ① - ⑥ of what to do and how to do it are the same (done for you on page 48)

⑦ List all the notes included in the printed brackets ⌞⎯⌟ printed below passage B
Indicate with curved brackets ⌒ notes which combine to form chords

Bar 1	B D G B D A* G B D G B F#* G E* A*	tonic	I
2	D B B D B D B D G G B D B D G B B D G	tonic	I
3	C G G C E G E C G G E	subdominant	IV
3	B G G B D G D B G G D	tonic	I
4	C G* E A C E C A E A	supertonic	II
4	D A F# A D C* D	dominant	V

* extra or passing notes

• match the notes you have just listed with the triad notes page 48 diagram column ⑥ opposite. Set them out clearly as shown below

  • bars 1 and 2 only tonic chord I has been used
    write Roman I at the start of each bracket, follow on with a line as shown

  • bar 3 first chord is IV   root position   below it write IV
          second chord is IV   1st inversion   below it write IVb
          third chord is I   1st inversion   below it write Ib
          fourth chord is I   2nd inversion   below it write Ic

  • bar 4 first chord is II   root position   below it write II
          second chord is II   1st inversion   below it write IIb
          third chord is V   root position   below it write V
          fourth chord is V   root position   draw a follow-on line as in bars 1 and 2

PROPER NAMES OF TRIAD NOTES

	SUPERTONIC				◆
	TONIC			□	
	LEADING NOTE				◆
	SUBMEDIANT		⊠	□	
V	DOMINANT	⊙			◆
IV	SUBDOMINANT		⊠	□	
	MEDIANT	⊙			
II	SUPERTONIC		⊠		
I	TONIC	⊙			

I	TONIC chord notes	⊙
II	SUPERTONIC chord notes	⊠
IV	SUBDOMINANT chord notes	□
V	DOMINANT chord notes	◆

- All triads use every-other-note structure

- Only one triad uses the leading note;
  only in minor keys does this
  pose any problem (see p. 45)

- **The proper names do not vary** — TONIC triads always use TONIC – MEDIANT – DOMINANT; DOMINANT triads always use DOMINANT – LEADING NOTE – SUPERTONIC; the same applies to supertonic and subdominant triads. Chord numbers are always I II IV V.

- **What do vary** are the notes to which the proper names refer, depending on the key / keys being studied

e.g. In key C the notes C E G are tonic, mediant, and dominant and form the *Tonic Triad* I.
  In key F the notes C E G are dominant, leading note, supertonic and form the *Dominant Triad* V.
  In key G the notes C E G are subdominant, submediant, tonic and form the *Subdominant Triad* IV.

- The same chords play different roles (do different jobs) in different places (rather like people)

- The root of a triad is the bottom letter-name of that triad
- the root is only the keynote (1st degree of the scale) if
  the bottom note of the triad is the tonic of the key
- in *all* the above examples the root of the triad is C,
  but only in *one* example is the root the keynote. Which one?

CADENCES — a cadence is simply 'an ending'

• chords are selected and used to help create certain musical effects
• *To end a piece of music convincingly* there are two types of *cadence chords* used

Chords used	Effect produced	Technical name
Dominant V moving to Tonic I	Final ending	Perfect cadence
Subdominant IV moving to Tonic I	Also Final ending	Plagal* cadence

* sometimes called 'Amen' cadence; used to be sung at the end of a hymn

• *To create an unfinished effect* halfway through a piece of music

Any chord I, II or IV to Dominant V	unfinished, pause	Imperfect cadence

• *To create and unexpected, surprise effect* in place of a perfect cadence

Dominant V to VI (or to a diminished or augmented chord)	unprepared for, strange or startling	Interrupted cadence

THE CADENTIAL $\frac{6}{4}$

• In perfect cadences the two last chords are always
  Dominant (usually root position) followed by *Tonic* (usually root position)

Key
A major

V I

The approach chord to these two (V, I) is very often Ic – tonic 2nd inversion figured $\frac{6}{4}$ and usually referred to as a <u>Cadential</u> $\frac{6}{4}$

• When the $\frac{6}{4}$ chord is used this way the figures $\frac{5}{3}$ are often printed under the following (dominant) bass note; the bottom note of the cadential $\frac{6}{4}$ is the same note, the figures indicate how the second chord follows the first. Sometimes the bass is one single note, or two tied notes. In this case the $\frac{5}{3}$ figures are needed.

• To our ears this particular chord progression is extremely familiar: on paper it is recognisable by the two dominant bass notes just before the end

In *Three blind mice!* and in *Baa - baa - black sheep . . .*

three blind mice!

lives down the lane!

• It is also commonly used as the main item in an *Imperfect Cadence*, often bar 4 in an 8 bar phrase (example below)

• questions about cadences and chord progressions ask for
  • CHORD IDENTIFICATION I II IV V in all keys, root positions and inversions
  • recognising a $\frac{6}{4}$ chord and its use as a cadential $\frac{6}{4}\frac{5}{3}$ on the dominant note only, in any key

• These questions give a passage of music and indicate which chords you must identify or look for. To answer them you need
  • to know the key of the music – whether major or minor
  • to know the *proper names* and which notes they refer to in that key
  • to recognise the appearance of root positions and inversions
  • to spot the *Dominant* bass note and locate any $\frac{6}{4}\frac{5}{3}$ progression

they also ask for CADENCE CHORD CHOICES in simple keys C G D F

• These questions consist of a short melody with groups of notes either numbered or lettered, requesting suitable suggestions for cadence chords (only using chords I II IV V). You need to
  • know the proper-names of the chords which form the cadences
  • decide the key, write the letter-names which form the 4 chords in that key.
  • write the letter-names of the notes in the groups, relate them to the four chords and decide which to use.

• Question: Suggest suitable chords at numbers 1, 2, 3, 4, 5 to form two cadences in the passage below. Name the cadences you choose. Use Roman Numerals for your answer and indicate any $\frac{6}{4}\frac{5}{3}$ progression if one is used.

• Key D: <u>Chord notes:</u>I   D F♯ A   II   E G B   IV   G B D   V   A C♯ E

• <u>Group notes</u>   1. B C♯ D B – IV   2. A – V   3. F♯ A – I   4. E A – V   5. D – I

• <u>Cadences</u>: Numbers 1 and 2, chords IV and V, Imperfect Cadence ending on dominant numbers 3, 4 and 5, chords I V I, the chords at numbers 3 and 4 should be Ic, then V ($\frac{6}{4}\frac{5}{3}$) with the dominant note in the bass. Chord at number 5 should be tonic root position. This makes a perfect cadence

Section VI
General Musicianship

OPEN and SHORT SCORE — vocal music

- Either score is clear for the singers to read (open is better)
- Short score is much better for the accompanist to read.

Open score   J. S. Bach

S.   [musical staff]   Soprano

A.   [musical staff]   Alto (contralto)

T.   [musical staff]   Tenor

B.   [musical staff]   Bass

The question will ask for a passage in one type of score to be transcribed to the other.

Short score   J. S. Bach

S.
A.   [musical staff]

T.
B.   [musical staff]

Transcribing short score to open score

- Soprano, Alto, Bass. Transfer each part to a separate stave in the correct order, keeping the pitch the same. Stalks up or down as appropriate to the position of the notes on the stave

- Tenor. Transpose the tenor part up an 8ve. Write it in the treble clef with a figure 8 below the clef sign. Stalks as appropriate to the position of the notes on the stave.

Transcribing open score to short score

- Soprano, alto. Transfer these parts to a single stave using a 𝄞 ; soprano above with stalks up, alto below with stalks down.

- Bass. Transfer this part to a stave with a 𝄢 . All stalks go downwards

- Tenor. Transpose the tenor part down an 8ve; write it on the same stave above the bass part, all stalks going upwards

Accidentals in short score

A ♯ or ♭ beside a note in one part in short score *must be written again* if it is needed for the same note sung by the other part on the same stave later in the bar.

Example

[musical staff]

C clefs ALTO and TENOR
• C clefs are so called because the signs for them indicate the position of *middle C*. The reason for their use is to reduce the need for the printing of leger lines which are hard to read; more importantly, they encroach upon space which could be needed by notes belonging to the stave above.

ALTO CLEF

used by violas

TENOR CLEF

used by cellos, bassoons, tenor trombones

• two bars from a cello study printed in the tenor clef; beneath are the same bars printed in the bass clef.
• the notes in the tenor clef are printed a 5th lower than those in the bass clef.

• Varied exercises using these clefs have been introduced into the Question section of this book — scales, intervals, triads, transpositions

The notes within the curved brackets } are identical in pitch

Key signature positions

Questions involving these clefs often take the form of:

Transcribing (keeping the pitch the same) from tenor to bass, alto to treble or vice versa
Transposing (at the octave*) from any clef to any other.

* means up or down an octave, whichever the question asks

TRANSPOSING INSTRUMENTS

The dictionary definition tells us:

"many wind instruments are built in fundamental tunings in which the major scale without a key signature (written as C major) actually sounds higher or lower. The names given to certain instruments (B♭ clarinet, cornet or trumpet in B♭, clarinet in A, horn in F, trumpet in F etc) indicate exactly how much higher or lower the instrument will sound in relation to the sound of C at concert pitch." [*Everyman's Dictionary of Music* — Eric Blom]

Instrument	The actual sounding pitch in relation to C written to sound at concert pitch	To sound at concert pitch the parts of these instruments must therefore be written	To *re-write* this music to sound at concert pitch it must be transposed
B♭ clarinet, cornet, trumpet	whole tone (major 2nd) below	whole tone (major 2nd) above concert pitch	down a whole tone (major 2nd)
clarinet in A	minor 3rd below	minor 3rd above concert pitch	down a minor 3rd
Horn in F	perfect 5th below	perfect 5th above concert pitch	down a perfect 5th
Trumpet in F	perfect 4th above	perfect 4th below concert pitch	up a perfect 4th

<u>Question</u>: This phrase ① is written for clarinet in A. *Transpose it **down** a minor 3rd* so that it will sound at concert pitch.

Remember to put the new key signature
*Transpose it **down** a minor 3rd* — not all exam questions tell you this.

Grieg: Peer Gynt

① **Alla marcia**

• If the printed phrase is written for a specific instrument, as this is for clarinet in A, it has been put up a minor 3rd specially for this instrument. For the phrase to sound at concert pitch when played by other, non-transposing instruments it must be put down a minor 3rd again.

<u>Question</u>: This passage ② for a horn in F is written at concert pitch. Rewrite it as it would be notated for the player *transpose it a perfect 5th higher*. Do not use a key signature but insert all necessary accidentals. Also add performance directions.

Tchaikovsky: Symphony no 5

② **Allegro con anima**

transpose it a perfect 5th higher These notes have been left at concert pitch; for a horn in F to sound right they must be played a perfect 5th higher than they are written here. Horns in F sound a perfect 5th lower than written pitch.

[Trumpets in F sound a *perfect 4th higher* than written pitch]

<u>A system for answering these and similar questions</u>

	Signature	Old key	Interval	New key	Signature
Phrase ①	B♭	F	Minor 3rd down	D	F♯ C♯
Phrase ②	F♯	G	Perfect 5th up	D	F♯ C♯

<u>First leave out all accidentals</u>

Phrase ①   • put new key signature – F♯ C♯ – put common time
                     • write all the notes a minor 3rd lower

Count down 3 letter-names –   old 1st note is D – D C B – new 1st note is B
                                          old 2nd note is E – E D C – new 2nd note is C etc. . . . .

Phrase ②   • do not put new key signature – put $\frac{6}{8}$ time
                     • write in all the notes a perfect 5th higher

Count up 5 letter-names –   old 1st note is D – D E F G A – new 1st note is A
                                      old 2nd note is C – C D E F G – new 2nd note is G etc. . . . .

Phrases ① and ②   • copy *all* performance directions

ACCIDENTALS: All accidentals must follow the same pattern as in the original (remember, an accidental lasts a whole bar)

Phrase ②
          • raise the 2nd note by a semitone (check with key signature)

Phrase ① Bar 2
          • 1st note – raised a semitone (check with key signature)
          • 3rd note – as 1st (still sharp)
          • 4th note – lowered
          • 5th note – lowered (check with key signature)

Here is a phrase written to sound at concert pitch, transposed for 4 different transposing instruments. Notice

- the keys change according to the instruments (see p. 56)
- all the intervals are exactly the same distance apart
- all the accidentals relate to the signatures to produce the same effect

Concert pitch: key D minor

Clarinet in B♭:
up a tone: key E minor

Clarinet in A:
up a minor 3rd: key F minor

Horn in F:
up a perf. 5th: key A minor

Trumpet in F:
down a perf. 4th: key A minor

- Work through the following practice phrases — 3 for each instrument
- Name each key. Check the accidentals carefully

Concert pitch
Key . . . . .   Key . . . . .   Key . . . . .

up a tone for Clarinet in B♭
Key . . . . .   Key . . . . .   Key . . . . .

Concert pitch
Key . . . . .   Key . . . . .   Key . . . . .

up a minor 3rd for Clarinet in A
Key . . . . .   Key . . . . .   Key . . . . .

Concert pitch
Key . . . . .   Key . . . . .   Key . . . . .

up a perfect 5th for Horn in F
Key . . . . .   Key . . . . .   Key . . . . .

Concert pitch
Key . . . . .   Key . . . . .   Key . . . . .

down a perfect 4th for Trumpet in F
Key . . . . .   Key . . . . .   Key . . . . .

MODULATION

This is the technique of changing key during the course of a piece of music. In order for a smooth shift to be made from the orbit of one key-note to that of a different one, accidentals must be introduced. If these are skilfully chosen their effect will be to transfer audience awareness logically into the environs of the desired new key; as long as the accidental(s) continue to be used the new key will seem like home. Modulation brings freedom from the confines of the major / minor key system: over the centuries composers have developed their own recognisable styles for exploring this technique.

RECOGNISING MODULATIONS

The most straightforward modulations are those to closely related keys: dominant (V), sub-dominant (IV), relative minor (VI in a major key), relative major (III in a minor key). Check through these simple examples. Study them for clues – new leading-notes are the most likely. Play them: hear the effect of the accidentals.

• Not all accidentals suggest modulations. In the question and answer below D♯ and D♮ (bar 1) and B♯ and B♮ (bar 2) have not been considered. Why? . . . .

Question: "In the extract below name the major key indicated by the key signature; if in your opinion any of the accidentals used suggests a modulation, give a reason and name the key"

Key . . . .

Answer:
New key E major (final note)
Reason: Repeated use of D♯ in bars 5, 6, & 7. It is the *leading note* for key E

ORNAMENTS

Sign	Name	Written out as played
	TURNS	(four or five note ornaments)
*	**turn** written over the note	*(musical notation)* or *(musical notation)*
	inverted turn	*(musical notation)* or *(musical notation)*
	turn written after the note	*(musical notation)* (turn played in 2nd ½ of beat)
	turn written over a dot. Here a triplet is used.	*(musical notation)*
	MORDENTS	(three note ornaments)
	mordent	*(musical notation)*
	sharpened mordent	*(musical notation)*
	inverted mordent	*(musical notation)*
	flattened inverted mordent	*(musical notation)*
	ACCIACCATURA takes up little or no time	*(musical notation)* ...*or simply* *(musical notation)*
	APPOGGIATURA written as *half* the note, takes *half* the time	*(musical notation)*
	TRILL variable number of next-door notes: usually ends with a turn	*(musical notation)*

two note ornaments

* the accidental affects the note above or below the main note, according to where it is printed

- The question will ask you to recognise and name written-out ornaments and to replace them with the appropriate signs.
- Turns and trills can vary how they look
  - turns always make a *curled* shape round the main note
  - trills are always two notes alternating more or less rapidly; the speed of the trill depends on the style of the music
- The other three are quite easy to recognise (learn how to spell them!)
- Questions relating to ornaments are included in the General Musicianship Questions pages 105-8

INTRODUCTION TO ANALYSIS

CANON

Thomas Tallis 1560

INTRODUCTION TO ANALYSIS

Musical analysis involves studying the facts about a piece of music; observing the type of materials used and the style in which the composer uses them.
- Tallis's canon is a well-known choral piece. It can be sung a capella (unaccompanied) or with organ or piano.
- Here it is written in short score. A 'canon' is similar to a round.

Melodic material
- four lines of melody pitched suitably for soprano. alto, tenor, bass
- straightforward construction of next-door notes and easily pitched intervals
- the tenor voice exactly copies the soprano melody, starting four beats later *
- the alto and bass lines are different, enriching and strengthening the two upper parts

Harmonic material
- on every beat note the voices combine to form a diatonic chord
- all are four-note chords – triad notes with one doubled, or with one extra note
- nineteen of the 32 chords are in root position

Rhythmic material
- unvaried crotchets are used throughout
- the phrases all start together on an up-beat: breathing places coincide
- the piece starts with an anacrusis (see Information Desk)

General observations / opinions
- the piece is in key G, there are no accidentals and no modulations
- each phrase starts on the tonic chord and ends on a tonic root position
- the four-square limitations of this music are worth commenting on: composers writing in the contrapuntal style of this period – Tallis was one of the most inspired – were masters in the art of subtly interweaving choral melodies, overlapping ends of phrases, changing keys, varying rhythms to please the sophisticated singers and audiences of their day. This piece would be very easy to perform by an inexperienced choir.

PENTATONIC & WHOLE TONE SCALES

Pentatonic scale uses five notes only, the intervals of which correspond to the black notes on a piano. Many Scottish songs, Chinese and Japanese tunes and African and Indian tribal songs use this scale.

Whole tone scale is formed of six whole tones. The subtly coloured atmospheric and dramatic effects which can be achieved by the use of this scale appealed strongly to Debussy (1862-1918), who fully explored its potential. He was the founder of the Impressionist school of composition during the early 20th century.

Musical mood is partly determined by the notes of the chosen scale. It is interesting that the pentatonic scale does not make use of the tritone (augmented 4th); the difficulty of pitching this interval and its awkward sound earned it the name "devil's interval". In early church music its use was sternly discouraged.

TWELVE NOTE MUSIC (serial music, atonal music)

- is a relatively modern system based on the mathematical fact of semitonal equality.
- In place of diatonic scales composers use chromatic scales (12 semitones).
- The notes are treated as equals and composers create series of tone-rows, in which every sound can have the same tonal rights as every other sound; there is no dominant, leading-note, tonic – a totally democratic system.
- In the early 20th century Schönberg, Webern and Alban Berg were the pioneers of atonal music.

MODAL MUSIC

- The modal system was the tonal basis of the earliest Greek music (400 CE onwards) and of all Western religious and secular music through to the 16th century , when the major / minor key system gradually became universal.
- After centuries of modified usage, the following is a workable definition:
  - six modes of eight notes each: starting notes correspond to C D E F G A
  - each mode is named after an ancient Greek province
  - the different mood of each is determined by the relative positions of the two semitones (see below)

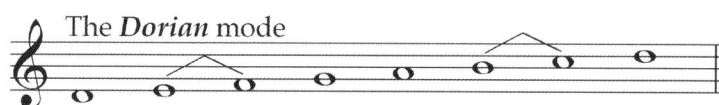

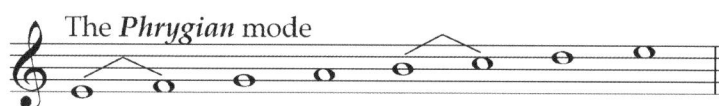

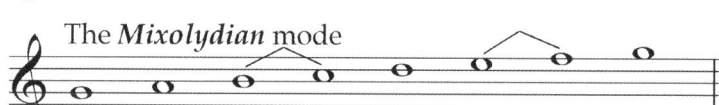

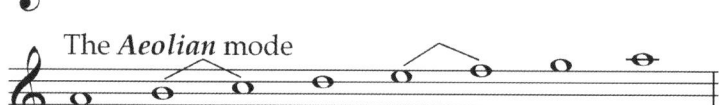

- semi-tones are marked

- play each mode, hear the different effects

- notice the *Ionian* mode is the major scale of C

- the *Aeolian* mode is the melodic minor scale of A without any raised leading note

- white note scale-patterns, intervals and triads can all be made part of modal composition

- it is an open-ended system with its own unique expressive potential

- it need not sound old-fashioned

PART II

Questions & Exercises
for practice

• many questions in Part II assume the possession of a manuscript book or pad

• a notice which should be printed on every page

READ THE QUESTION PROPERLY!!!

TIME PATTERNS — revision and practice

Fill up the bars below with a good variety of different groups and single notes or rests so that each bar adds up to the right number of beats. In the final bar of each line write a single note, or tied notes and/or rests to last the whole bar.

TO REMIND YOU . . . . .

• when *crotchets* are beats — some groups and notes to use

• when *dotted crotchets* are beats — some groups and notes to use

• decide <u>how many</u> of <u>which beat note</u> every exercise needs

Write the full description (simple / compound – duple, triple, quadruple, irregular) of the following time signatures, as shown

simple duple

TIME PATTERNS — continued

Fill up the bars with a variety of groups, single notes or rests so that each bar adds up to the right number of beats. On this page, when

♪ are beat notes, use

♩ are beat notes, use

♪. are beat notes, use

Write the full description (simple / compound – duple, triple, quadruple, irregular) of the following time signatures, as shown

$\frac{3}{8}$ *simple triple* $\qquad$ $\frac{4}{8}$

$\frac{7}{8}$ $\qquad$ $\frac{2}{2}$

$\frac{3}{2}$ $\qquad$ $\frac{4}{2}$

$\frac{6}{16}$ $\qquad$ $\frac{9}{16}$

$\frac{12}{16}$ $\qquad$ $\frac{5}{16}$

66 QUESTIONS

TIME and RHYTHM — giving types of question and practical systems for working
- add missing bar lines, time signatures and rests
- correct faulty groupings (beaming) of small notes
- re-write using notes of half/twice the value
- notice and insert changes of time signature

- Add missing bar lines — the piece starts on the first beat of a bar

— look at the time signature —
  - what is the beat note? — how many of them to a bar?
  - put faint pencil rings round every beats-worth of notes (as shown)
  - as the time signature indicates, count the beats, fill in the bar lines; ‖ at the end

- Add missing bar lines to the following passages which all start on the first beat of the bar.
  Time signatures given

• Add the missing time signature to the following short passages, and supply their full names
e.g. simple duple, compound triple

ⓐ

ⓑ

• count the crotchets — six in both ⓐ and ⓑ
• possibilities — 3 minim beats 𝅗𝅥 𝅗𝅥 𝅗𝅥 = 6, or 2 dotted minim beats 𝅗𝅥. 𝅗𝅥. = 6
• count six while clapping each rhythm in turn — feel the swing of the rhythm, decide where the accents come — how many to the bar

| **1** 2 **3** 4 **5** 6 | *three* beats |
| **1** 2 3 **4** 5 6 | *two* beats |

• test your decision by pencil rings

Answers: Time signatures ⓐ . . . . ⓑ . . . .   Descriptions ⓐ ....
ⓑ ....

• Add missing time signature

• count crotchets – pencil rings of *beamed groups* to decide the *beat note*, clap the rhythm
• find the simplest-looking bar — compare with the others — Decide
• Add missing time signatures to the following. Supply their full names.
(If 5 or 7 beats, write *Irregular*)

①

Name ....

②

Name ....

The Swan - Saint Saens

③

Name ....

④

Name ....

⑤

Name ....

TIES, TRIPLETS & DUPLETS

TIES:

- the value of a note or rest can be increased by a tie
- ♩ ♪ the first note is sounded and held for its length + that of the second note
- the time value of ♩ ♪ is the same as ♩.
- tied notes can span bar lines or half bar divisions

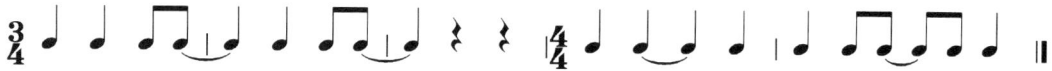

$$\frac{3}{4} \; \text{♩ ♩ ♩ ♫♩ ♩ ♩ ♫♩ ♩ ♩ 𝄾 𝄾} \quad \frac{4}{4} \; \text{♩ ♩♩ ♩ ♩ ♩ ♩ ♫♩ ♫♩ ♩} \; \|$$

- if asked to supply bar lines, a tie can be a useful indication:
  whole notes or dotted notes cannot span bar lines.

TRIPLETS and DUPLETS

TRIPLETS:

- in *simple time* beat notes divide by 2 ♩ = ♫   ♪ = ♬
- if three notes are wanted as an occasional or repetitive feature
  the beat note is divided into 3 ♩ = ♫♩ ⌊—3—⌋   ♪ = ♬♪ ⌊—3—⌋
- this group of three is called a triplet and always indicated by figure 3
- the presence of triplets is a clear indication that the music is in simple time
- triplets increase the number of notes in the beat division

DUPLETS:

- in *compound time* beat notes divide by 3 ♩. = ♫♩   ♩. = ♩ ♩ ♩
- if two notes are wanted (effective as a brake in a running passage)
  the beat note is divided into 2 ♩. = ♫ ⌊—2—⌋   ♩. = ♩ ♩ ⌊—2—⌋
- this group of two is called a duplet and always indicated by the figure 2
- the presence of duplets is a clear indication that the music is in compound time
- duplets decrease the number of notes in the beat division

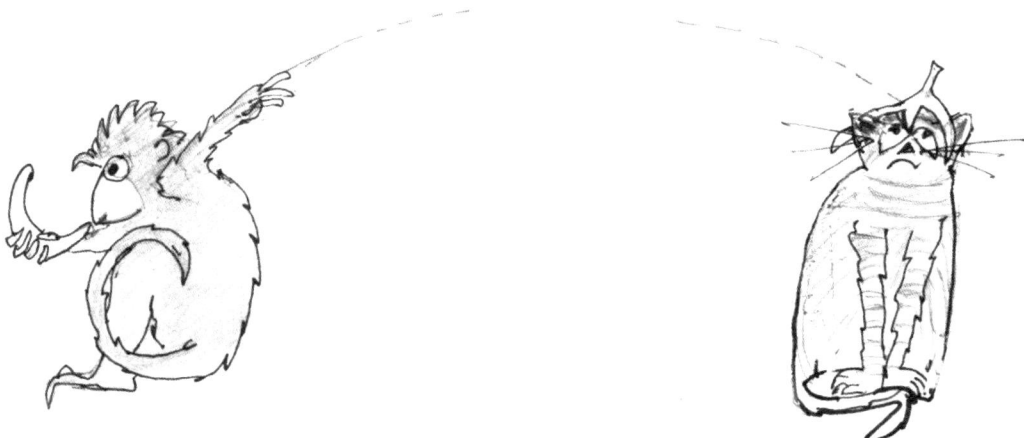

MORE COMPLEX

No obvious crotchet beats, possibly compound time, missing bar lines *and* signature

<u>Clues to compound time</u>

• several dotted notes or rests e.g.

• beamed groups of *three* corresponding to the value of the dotted notes

e.g.

• uneven groups of two, beamed or not, corresponding to the same value

e.g.

• even group(s) of two marked as a duplet e.g. worth

• add missing time signature; supply the full name of the signature

Name ....

• ring the beamed groups, these are beats, their value is 3 semiquavers each
• the last bar has a dotted note and a dotted rest, both valued at 3 semiquavers
• beat consists of ♪♪♪, the lower number of the signature is 16
• each bar contains two beats, value 6 semiquavers, the upper number is 6

• add missing time signatures *and* bar lines to these three passages.
  All start on the first beat of the bar

①
① • ring the *beamed groups* — these are beats. Decide their value
  • Crotchets. Put 4 at the bottom of the signature
  • count the crotchets-worth in the piece — 15
  • time signature can be $\frac{3}{4}$ (5 bars of 3 beats) or $\frac{5}{4}$ (3 bars of 5 beats)
  • decide by testing where it is possible to put the bar lines.

② • Beamed groups are *not* beats — they consist of two *and* three quavers — also single adjacent (next-door) quavers — also more quavers than any other note. These facts suggest *quavers* could be the beat note. Count them — test where the bar lines will best fit — put in the time signature.

③ • Study it for a likely beat note (*hint* — there are more minims than crotchets). Count them. Choose time signature to fit the bar line pattern.

②

③

70 QUESTIONS

add missing rests (marked by a *) to complete the following bars

- check the beat note. Ring all beats. If a note is worth more than a beat, write its value above it
- beneath each * write a rest of the exact time value
- when the * is part of a beamed group (bar 3) fit the rest within the group
- when the * is part of a beat and is followed by another * (bar 2) the rule is
  'finish the beat then finish the bar'. Do not write a single rest in place of two
- if rests and *bar lines* are both missing add the bar lines first
- if rests are needed for most of a bar
  in triple time   —   beats 1 & 2 should be written as one — not beats 2 & 3
  in quadruple time — beats 1 & 2 also 3 & 4 should be written as one — not beats 2 & 3

Add missing rests at the places marked *

Add missing barlines and rests marked * to the following three-bar phrases.
Both start on the first beat of the bar

CORRECTING FAULTY GROUPS first revise standard grouping

Beat notes	SIMPLE TIME								

• there can be other patterns — different placing of rests — ties may be used

COMPOUND TIME

• correct the grouping (beaming) of notes in this passage

• check the beat (crotchet). Ring the beats and beam them. Also beam any odd pairs of small notes worth less than a beat (bar 4)

• **N.B.** In quadruple time (as this is) if the *first two* or *last two* beats of a bar can be beamed together they should be. Bar ② last two beats, bar ③ first two beats, bar ④ last two beats

• Here's how it should look

• Rewrite the following passages grouping the notes correctly

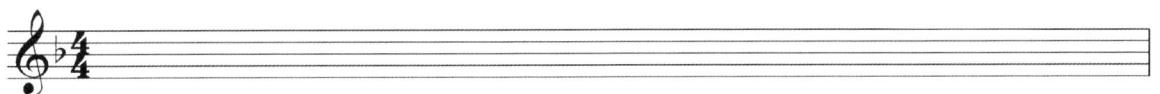

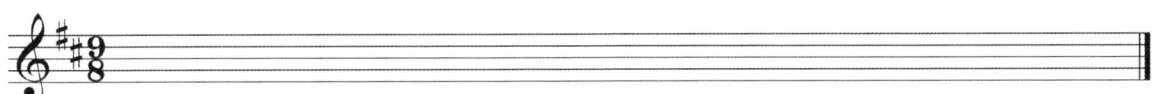

DOUBLING OR HALVING NOTE VALUES
without altering the original rhythmic shape

• alter the note values in this rhythm so as to *double* their value.

• change the time signature. *Double* the beat note by *halving the bottom number*
• *Double* every note and rest
• Leave any dots in place

• Rewrite the following using notes and rests of *double the length*. Change the time signatures to suit

• alter the note values in this rhythm so as to *halve* their value

• change the time signature. *Halve* the beat note by .... (you guessed it!) Leave the top number unchanged.
• halve every note and rest. Notice that when two crotchets ♩ ♩ are halved (e.g. bar ②) and become two quavers ♪ ♪ they should be beamed together: also the first three notes in bar ④

• Rewrite the following using notes and rests *half the length*. Change the time signatures to suit

CHANGING TIME SIGNATURES during a piece of music
• Insert any necessary changes of time signature in the following

• most of the notes are quavers so use them as counters
• bars ① and ③ have identical rhythms and notes .... put $\frac{6}{8}$ in bar 3

• bars ④ and ⑦ both have seven quavers .... put $\frac{7}{8}$ in both

• bar ⑥ has 6 quavers and looks like 2 beats of compound time put $\frac{6}{8}$

• bar ② also has 6 quavers, but looks more like simple time .. put $\frac{3}{4}$

• bar ⑤ has 5 quavers... put $\frac{5}{8}$

In general   • if a bar seems harder to classify, using
                   • different notes as counters
                   • more complex rhythm patterns

        • systematically list what is in the bar –
          ring any small rhythm groups, find their value
        • test various simple / compound time requirements
        • there will be a time signature which fits

In the following 4 extracts some bars need different time signatures.

Write these at the places marked *

74 QUESTIONS

IRREGULAR GROUPINGS

- Composers sometimes use scattered groups or flurries of small notes which *do not exactly fit mathematically* into the counting system

- They have to be made to fit into a time-slot so that players can perform the music with a steady rhythm

- above or below each group of random notes there will be a printed number. If it is 7, 6 or 5 the little notes will be printed with the same note values as a set of 4
  e.g.

  will both be played fast enough to fit into the time-slot of
  (in fact one crotchet)

- if the printed number is 9 or above the little notes will be printed with the same note values as a set of 8

  played to fit   same time-slot as   again, one crotchet's worth

  played to fit   N.B. bigger notes used same time-slot as   one minim's worth

Question: Supply the missing rests (marked *) and barlines to the given extract, which begins on the first beat of the bar

- 4 crotchets to the bar (time signature) — use the blank stave for workings

- pencil rings round all crotchets (if 2 write 2) — put bar lines in

- the 5 group are worth 4 demisemiquavers, one ♪ — the * *must be* the other quaver ⌐

- the ♪ * ♪ must be a ⌐

- final * must be ▬ minim rest

- the bar lines work out exactly

Add the time signatures to the following extracts.
Underneath write the correct time description e.g. compound duple, simple triple etc

Description...

Description...

Description...

Description...

Description...

76 QUESTIONS

WRITING MAJOR SCALES to given specifications. Work in your manuscript book

- Read each question carefully —
  check clef, key, note values, scale direction. In all answers mark semitones thus

- Take care positioning the note stalks. Use the *At-a-Glance* chart page 28

Question: Write the following major scales with key signatures

𝄞 D, minims, ascending   𝄞 E♭, crotchets, ascending   𝄢 G, minims, descending

𝄢 B crotchets, ascending   𝄢 D♭, minims, descending   𝄞 F crotchets descending

Question: Write the following major scales without key signatures. Add the necessary sharps or flats in front of the notes they refer to

𝄞 E, minims, ascending,   𝄞 A♭, crotchets, descending   𝄢 F♯, minims, descending

𝄢 B♭, crotchets, ascending   𝄢 A, minims, descending   𝄞 D crotchets, descending

Question: Write the following major scale with key signatures using the given rhythm

𝄞 A♭, ascending   𝄢 D, descending   𝄞 B♭, descending

𝄢 G♭, descending   𝄞 D♭, ascending   𝄢 F, ascending

Question: Write the following major scales without key signatures using the given rhythm

𝄞 E, descending   𝄞 B, ascending   𝄢 E♭, ascending

𝄢 A♭, ascending   𝄢 D♭, descending   𝄞 G♭, ascending

Question: Write the following major scales without key signatures to the given rhythm in the required clefs

In the tenor clef, ascending
    G, F, D

In the tenor clef, descending
    C, A, E

In the alto clef, ascending
    B♭, C, A

In the also clef, descending
    G, D♭, F

WRITING HARMONIC MINOR SCALES
Again — read each question carefully
Remember: • all minor key signatures flatten the 3rd, 6th and 7th notes of the scale, either by *using flats* against them or by *not using sharps*
    • harmonic minor scales use the same scale notes both up and down

If using a key signature, this will flatten the leading note which will always need an accidental to raise it

*if **not** using a key signature*
        • in keys which use sharps; once these have been added the 7th (leading notes) will still need accidentals to raise them
        • in keys which use flats; once these have been added, only two scales, **D minor** and **G minor**, each need a sharp on the 7th note. All the other leading notes remain as naturals and need no accidentals
        • **A minor** uses neither sharps nor flats; it needs a sharp on the 7th note

Question: Write the following harmonic minor scales with key signatures using the given rhythm

    D min ascending   E min descending   G min ascending

    B min descending   A minor ascending

Question: Write the following harmonic minor scales without key signatures using the given rhythm

    C min ascending   F♯ min descending   F min ascending

    B♭ min descending   C♯ min ascending

Question: Write the following harmonic minor scales with key signatures in the required clefs. Invent a rhythm in common time. Mark the semitones ⌃

    Tenor clef, C min ascending   Alto clef, F min descending

    Alto clef, G♯ min ascending   Tenor clef, C♯ minor descending

Question: Write the following harmonic minor scales without key signatures in the required clefs. Invent a rhythm in ⁶⁄₈ time. Mark the semitones ⌃

    Alto clef, C♯ min descending   Tenor clef, F♯ min ascending

    Alto clef, A min ascending   Tenor clef, B♭ minor descending

WRITING MELODIC MINOR SCALES — careful reading of questions is still needed

GOING UPWARDS
- *If using a key signature* the 6th and 7th degrees of the scale will always require accidentals to raise them

- *If **not** using a key signature*
  - in keys which use sharp key signatures; once these have been added, both the 6th and 7th notes will require accidentals to raise them
  - in keys which use flat key signatures; once these have been added, two scales only, D minor and G minor, require one accidental each to raise the 7th note. Because of the absence of the key signature
    - the 6th note in these 2 keys   } do not require
    - the 6th and 7th notes in the other flat keys } any accidentals
  - A minor should be treated as a sharp key — raise the 6th and 7th notes

GOING DOWNWARDS
- follow the key signature indications. Do *not* raise the 7th note

GOING UP AND DOWN
- indicate, by means of accidentals if necessary, which notes are to be played

Question: Write the following melodic minor scales ascending in the required clefs. Use a key signature and the given rhythm

E min   D min   Tenor clef, G min   Alto clef, B min

Tenor clef, C min   Alto clef, F♯ min   B♭ min

Question: Write the following melodic minor scales ascending. Do not use a key signature. use the required clefs and invent a rhythm in $\frac{4}{4}$ time

C min   B min   Alto clef, B♭ min

Tenor clef, C♯ min   G min   D min

Question: Write the required melodic minor scales descending. Use a key signature. Invent a rhythm in $\frac{3}{4}$ time

Alto clef, E♭ min   Tenor clef, F min   F♯ min

G♯ min   Alto clef, A min   Tenor clef, E min

MELODIC MINOR SCALES continued

Question: In the required key and using the indicated key signatures write the following melodic
  minor scales both ascending and descending. Use all semibreves.

    🎼 3 flats   🎼: 3 sharps   tenor clef 2 flats

    alto clef 4 sharps   🎼: 5 flats   tenor clef 5 sharps

Question: Write the following melodic minor scales both ascending and descending. Do not use a
  key signature; write all notes as semibreves

    🎼 G min   🎼: B min   tenor clef F♯ min

    Alto clef, A min   🎼: D min   🎼 F min

WRITING CHROMATIC SCALES

- RULE   use one note for each letter name on the 1st, 5th and 8th degrees of the scale. Use two
  notes for all the other letter names (see example below)

- METHOD   list the letter names, number them *from the bottom upwards.*
  Set them out on the stave (13 notes in all)
  Write accidentals to sound each semitone (Use Keyboard Picture Starters page 1)

Question: Write chromatic scales using the given clefs and starting notes. Follow the direction
  indicated and use all semibreves.

    🎼 A, descending (example shown below)   Alto clef, F# descending

    Tenor clef, Eb, ascending   🎼: G ascending   🎼 Bb ascending

    Alto clef, F, descending   Tenor clef, E, descending   🎼: D, ascending

Example

A descending

Name the keynotes of the following passages

METHOD   List the accidentals used in each passage (in the correct order)

• If they are *all sharps* — the key can be major or minor. The sharpest note will be the leading note.
  Relate your findings to the *At-a-Glance* chart on page 28

Example of all sharps — F C G D B — the sharpest note is B which is the leading note for key C♯
minor, key signature F C G D. This matches the passage which ends on C♯

• If they are *all flats* — the key will be major; the key note will be the last flat but one.
  Possible exception — if the piece *ends* on the minor key note which uses these flats and the use of
  the leading note has been avoided, check with the two key notes which use this signature.

• If they are a mixture — flats and sharps or flats and naturals — the key will be *minor*, the sharpest
  note will be the leading note.

Remember — double sharps are the sharpest, then sharps, then naturals

Remember — the last note is *not always* the key note

WRITING AND RECOGNISING INTERVALS

Question: Above the given notes write a second note to make the named intervals

| perf 5th | min 9th | min 3rd | maj 6th | min 7th | aug 4th | dim 5th | maj 2nd | perf 12th | dim 7th |

Question: Below the given notes write a second note to make the named intervals

| perf 4th | min 9th | min 6th | maj 6th | perf 5th | dim 5th | maj 7th | maj 2nd | min 10th | aug 4th |

Question: Give the number and description of the following intervals

Question: Using notes in the major key using this signature write the following intervals

| perf 5th | maj 6th | min 7th | aug 4th | maj 3rd | min 2nd | maj 9th |

Question: Name one key in which each of these intervals could occur

Key ___

Key ___

82 QUESTIONS

WRITING and RECOGNISING INTERVALS

Question: Name, invert and re-name the following intervals.
Give the descriptive as well as the numerical name: e.g. — major 6th, augmented 4th etc

Name —— ——— ——— ——— ——— ——— ———

Invert

Rename —— ——— ——— ——— ——— ——— ———

WRITING and IDENTIFYING TRIADS

READ THE QUESTIONS CAREFULLY

Question: Write tonic triads in root position in the following keys. Use accidentals where needed,
not key signatures

D maj   B maj   Bb min   Eb maj   G# min   Ab maj   F min   C# min   F# maj   Db maj

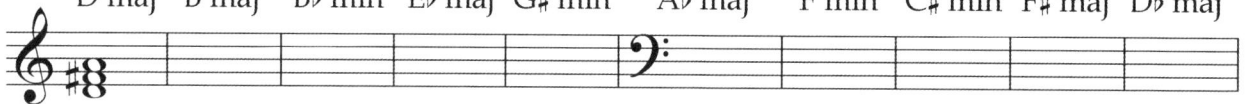

Question: With reference to the given key signatures, name the keys and the following triads using
Roman numerals. All are in root position.

Key . . . . .   Key . . . . .   Key . . . . .

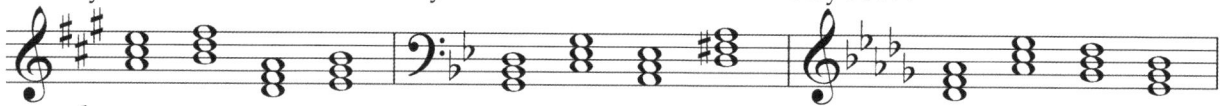

Numerals — — — —   — — — —   — — — —

Question: Identify the bass notes of the following triads by writing root — third — fifth as
appropriate. The key is E major

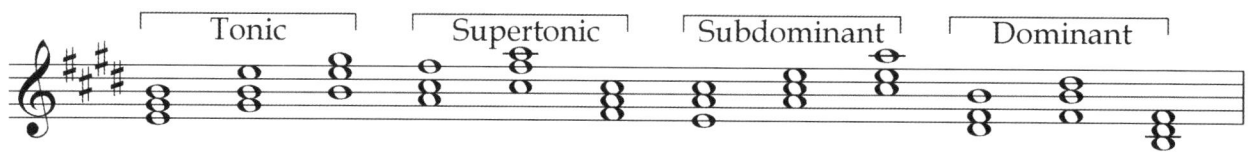

—— ——— ——— ——— ——— ——— ——— ———

WRITING and IDENTIFYING TRIADS (Contd)

Question: Identify the *bass notes* of the following triads using this method

root in the bass
root position } write **(a)**

third in the bass
first inversion } write **(b)**

fifth in the bass
second inversion } write **(c)**

letters (a), (b) or (c)

Question: Identify the bass notes of the following triads by using figures
- if root position, leave blank
- if 1st inversion write **6**
- if 2nd inversion write **6 4**

numbers

Question: In the key of D major write the following triads in the positions indicated

I   Ib   IV   IIb   Ic   V   I

Question: In the key of Eb major write the following triads in the positions indicated.
Use a key signature

Supertonic
1st inversion

Tonic
2nd inversion

Dominant
root position

Tonic
Root position

Question: In the following passage mark ⌐¬ the two chords which form the Cadential **6 4**. These are **Ic** and **V** next door to each other. The piece is in key G

WRITING and IDENTIFYING CHORDS

Question: In the treble clef write the triads indicated. In the bass clef repeat the root of each triad
(4 notes in all — see example below). The question is in key F.

Example in key C

Question: key F

Question: Add key signatures. Name the five triads, state the position of each and whether it is
major or minor. In the bass clef write the root of each triad (example no. 1 below)

IDENTIFYING CHORDS, TRANSCRIBING SHORT TO OPEN SCORE

Question: Name the keys in the following short score passages. Identify the chords marked * and
state the position of each chord — IVb, II, Ib etc. In your manuscript book transcribe them
into open score.

KEYS, CHORDS, OPEN and SHORT SCORE

Question: Name the keys in the following short score passages. Identify the chords marked * and
state the position of each chord (V, IIb etc). In your manuscript book transcribe them into
open score.

A

Carol

B

Key____ ....

Key____ ....

C

Farnaby

Key____ ....

A useful system for identifying key-related triads and chords

FIRST
• check key note. In minor keys the sharpest note (accidental) will be the leading note. If there is no
signature, list the accidentals and compare with the *At-a-Glance* chart.

• having decided the key, write the scale letter names going upwards beside the proper names.
From this list jot down (starting at the bottom)
  • the letter names which form the triads I, II, IV, V. In a minor key the 3rd in triad V will need to
    be raised by an accidental. Check with the key signature.
  • compare your letter names with those of the required triads or chords

CADENTIAL PROGRESSIONS

Question: Suggest suitable cadential progressions in the following four melodies by indicating one
chord at each of the places marked A - E. Use as your method of indication *either* Roman
numerals *or* letter names, *or* by writing notes on the staves. Do not indicate chord
positions.

1.

A   B   C   D   E

A ____ B____   C____ D____ E____

CADENTIAL PROGRESSIONS contd

Question: Using the same four melodies above, write the proper names (tonic, dominant etc.) for the chords you have chosen at letters C, D and E. Also, give the number of the melody in which the use of figures $\begin{smallmatrix}6 & 5 \\ 4 & 3\end{smallmatrix}$ (a cadential $\begin{smallmatrix}6 \\ 4\end{smallmatrix}$) beneath chords C and D would be suitable.

Melody Nos.

1.   chord C.....................................chord D.....................................chord E.....................................

2.   chord C.....................................chord D.....................................chord E.....................................

3.   chord C.....................................chord D.....................................chord E.....................................

4.   chord C.....................................chord D.....................................chord E.....................................

Cadential $\begin{smallmatrix}6 \\ 4\end{smallmatrix}$ at the end of melody number . . . . . .

TRANSCRIBING and TRANSPOSING

Question: Transcribe the following passage into short score. Add all necessary directions. Use your manuscript book.

The opening of *Come, Phyllis, come*, a Jacobean part song by Thomas Ford (1580 – 1648)

TRANSPOSING INSTRUMENTS B♭, F, A

Question: This passage is written for clarinet in B♭. Transpose it down as it will sound at concert pitch (a major 2nd lower). Use your manuscript book.

Keep a place for me

Question: This passage is written for horn in F. Write it out as it will sound at concert pitch (a perfect 5th lower). Insert key and time signatures and performance directions.

TRANSPOSING INSTRUMENTS continued

Question: Transpose this passage up a perfect 5th so that it will sound at concert pitch when played
by a horn in F. Do not use a key signature but add accidentals only before the notes that
need them.

Question: This passage is written at concert pitch. Rewrite it as it would be notated for a clarinet in
A (transpose it a minor 3rd higher).

TRANSCRIPTION in ALTO and TENOR CLEFS

Question: rewrite these passages at the same pitch, using the clefs indicated. Include performance
directions.

In questions involving changing clef while keeping the pitch the same
 • locate middle C (or nearest note) in the given passage
 • transfer it to the new stave in the correct place
 • relate to this note, calculating intervals to / from it

TRANSCRIPTIONS at pitch, at the octave

Question: transcribe the passage below into the alto clef, keeping the pitch the same.

*Read this question carefully — middle C must go down one octave as well as all the other notes

Question: transpose the following passage down an octave into the bass clef

ALTO, TENOR CLEF-RELATED QUESTIONS

Question: write the following triads with key signatures.

① ② ③ ④ ⑤

dominant	sub-dominant	supertonic	tonic	dominant
Key: B minor	Key: G♭ major	Key: E major	Key: G♯ minor	Key: F minor

Question: add the correct clefs and key signatures to make the scales named below. Add any extra accidentals needed.

B melodic minor

D♭ major

F harmonic minor

MODULATION

Question: name the keys, stating major or minor, to which these passages modulate. Also name the
original key and the accidental largely responsible for the changed key note.

Key.........   New key..............accidental..........

Key.........   New key..............accidental..........

Key.........   New key..............accidental..........

Key.........   New key..............accidental..........

Key.........   New key..............accidental..........

Question: name the keys of the following short passages. Some of the accidentals used suggest
new key notes; at each star * add the key note suggested, using a note of the correct
time value.

Key.........   *

Key.........   *

Key.........   *

Key.........   *

Key.........   *

CREATIVE STUDY

just what I needed — a lovely smooth, clean sheet of new manuscript paper

• Sometimes original themes and rhythms come 'out of the blue' into your head. If an instrument is handy you can pick the tunes out, maybe with triads and chords to match – or play a rhythm on the drums

• If you want to write it down . . . . . .

. . . . . . this is when you will need some of the • notes • key and time signatures • triads • rhythms • intervals • chords • clefs • scales • modes • accidentals . . . . . all of which you have so carefully studied

• the next five pages contain logically worked out key and rhythm plans as study aids for composing rhythms and melodies — helpful like technical drawings are to a builder

The two pages *Approach to Modal Music* suggest
• write a lyric; choose one of the 6 modes (page 62)
• play them — each one is unique, an attractive feature which could make the creation of an original designer-based end-product more possible . . . . . .

• also try imaginative experiments with ways of realising your song. Relate the lyric to the visual arts — use patterns and shapes, — curved, straight or zigzag lines — colours, textures — shape these to the words — how many in a phrase — their mood — their rise and fall —

• for your song to be readable and singable, you'll be glad of your careful study

WRITING RHYTHMS — as for DRUMS

Question: Write an 8-bar rhythm in 𝟤/𝟤 time. Include this note ♩·· *

* a double-dotted note. The first dot adds half the value of the note; the second dot adds half the value of the first dot.

Example: ♩·· = ♩⏜♪·♪

METHOD
• Space out eight bar lines and number the bars as shown

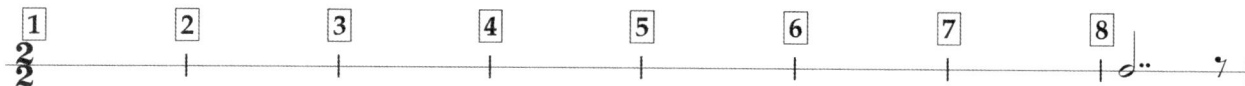

[1]   [2]   [3]   [4]   [5]   [6]   [7]   [8]
𝟤/𝟤

• Every bar *must contain two minims-worth*. Remind yourself of the *standard groupings* (see p. 71)

• *A useful tip:* Put one long note in bar 8.   ♩·· is worth the whole bar with a 𝄾 added.
  It would be a good place for it.

• *A quick formula:*   ✿ make bars 1 and 3 and 7 the same pattern
                         ✿ make bars 5 and 6 the same pattern (different from 1, 3, and 7)
                         ✿ make bar 2 different; make bar 4 straight beat notes

EXAMPLE

• Clap this pattern   ✿ you can hear a *logical shape* in the 8-bar sequence
                       ✿ *repeated rhythms* create continuity as the bars follow on
                       ✿ the purpose of the *two long notes* half way (bar 4) is to balance the phrase as
                         a unit, moving steadily towards the long note in bar 8
                       ✿ the *triplet* in bar 2 has been picked out and used as a feature in bars 5 and 6

• Many people can imagine and hear rhythms (and tunes) in their heads. Whether you can or not,
  it's useful to know how to construct a tidy, accurate, well-balanced rhythm

• One thing to avoid – introducing lots of different rhythm patterns to prove you understand them.
  Use a few, repeat them is a better plan.

Question: Write an 8-bar rhythm to the given words. Add tempo directions

"How can I learn to train a dog
If I haven't got a dog to train?"

METHOD
• Say the words and clap for the more important ones. Underline these: they are the ones which could and/or should be accented

| **How** can I | **learn** to | **train** a | **dog**
If I | **have**n't got a | **dog** to | **train**?

• Draw a line in front of each underlined word as shown: these are bar lines

• The question asks for '8 bars'. There are only 7 underlined words. An extra bar must be added, as shown. The final note will need to be tied between bars 7 and 8 (as shown).

• Write the accented words to the *right of each bar line*. Fit the other words in.

| 1 **How** can I | 2 **learn** to | 3 **train** a | 4 **dog** if I |

| 5 **have**n't got a | 6 **dog** to | 7 **train**? . . . | 8 . . . . ||

• Choose a time signature; experiment clapping some rhythms

EXAMPLE

Either of these
would fit.

• $\frac{2}{4}$ gives a positive on-going message: "Why isn't anyone buying me a dog?"

• $\frac{3}{4}$ is less pushy, more persuasive: "Maybe I can talk them round . . . ?"

• Choose which you want, set it out tidily, with the words written *exactly* below the notes which belong to them. Work at first in pencil — this makes slight adjustments possible

EXAMPLE
• in $\frac{2}{4}$ time there are three bars of *even crotchets* — bars 2, 3, & 6
Try the effect of 'dots and tails (T & R p. 18) on some or all of these three bars

• in the $\frac{3}{4}$ version, bar 4, three even crotchets might seem dull — varied length notes could be better

• the even crotchets are not wrong: the varied versions show the word meanings more clearly

• *Suitable tempo directions.* Study the MUSICAL TERMS section to find "le mot juste" (French for "exactly the right word.")

94 CREATIVE STUDY

WRITING A MELODY FOR A NAMED INSTRUMENT

Compose a melody for a violin, flute or clarinet, using the given opening. Indicate the tempo and other performance directions, including any which may be required for the instrument chosen. The complete melody should not be more than 8 bars long.

Chosen instrument: VIOLIN

- exactly 8 bars is easiest. Space them out and number them. End with a double bar line

METHOD (always work in pencil first)

- Plan the rhythm. Pencil it in faintly above the bars. (You can use the *quick formula* p. 92) Revise 'Standard groupings' (see p. 71)

- Plan the MELODY. Decide the key (See *At-a-Glance* chart p. 28) B♭ major or G minor — which?

bar 1	all given notes but one are the tonic triad of G minor — G, B♭, D
bar 2	most given notes are the dominant triad of G minor. The F♯ (raised leading note) is the clearest possible indication for the key to be G minor
bar 8	put key note G, either 2 beats (♩.) or one beat and a beat's rest — as shown
bar 4	(half way bar) select 2 notes of the dominant triad (D F♯ A) — as shown
bar 3	must take the melody from C (last note of bar 2) to A (first note of bar 4). Pencil in a convenient route — as shown
bar 5	should start up near top D (last note of bar 4)
bars 5 & 6	plan to relate these two bars by using *sequential phrases*. These employ the same rhythms, same shaped tonal patterns, *different* notes
bar 7	the last note could be the leading note; before that the dominant. The three first notes could imitate the last three of bar 6

String Playing
Down bow ⊓ usual on a first-beat opening note.
Up bow ∨ for an up-beat opening, or for a phrase starting on a weak beat (e.g. bar 4)
Legato is indicated by slurs
Staccato is indicated by dots
Performance directions:
choose suitable (foreign) words suggesting tempo and style.
Study the dynamic markings suggested

WRITING RHYTHMS and MELODIES

Question: write three 8 bar rhythms using the given openings and endings

Next write three 8 bar melodies in the keys indicated by the signatures using the given openings and the rhythms you have just written above. Use the dominant or notes of the dominant chord in bar 4. Supply performance directions (style and tempo, dynamic indications)

Question: write two 4 bar rhythms using the given time signatures and including the given rhythmic patterns

a) in 3/4 time. Include

b) in 6/8 time. Include

96 CREATIVE STUDY

WRITING A MELODY TO GIVEN WORDS

Compose a melody for the following words. Write each syllable under the note or notes to which it is to be sung. Indicate tempo and other performance directions as appropriate. Maximum 8 bars

"December" The Bellman's Song
Cold December has set in; the poor man's back is clothen'd thin:
The trees are bare, the birds are mute: the pot and toast will very well suit.

METHOD

- **Planning the rhythm** (see *write an 8 bar rhythm to given words* p. 93)

  - Underline strong words and put bar lines in front

  |Cold December |has set in; the |poor man's back is | clothen'd thin:
  The |trees are bare, the |birds are mute: the |pot and toast will |very well suit.

  - Set out 8 bars, write the words under as asked. (This is a man's song: use the bass clef)

Cold De-cem-ber has set in; the poor man's back is cloth-en'd thin: The
trees are bare, the birds are mute: the pot and toast will ver-y well suit.

  - number the bars

  - choose a time signature and rhythm pattern. The bellman or watchman will sing as he walks along, confident, unhurried

  - Experiment with clapping to the words

Cold   De-cem-ber   has   set   in;   the *etc.*

  Common time $\frac{4}{4}$ would suit this very well. Try some others if you wish.

  - Even beat-notes, very simply varied by dots and tails (see T & R, p. 18) provide an acceptable rhythmic structure upon which to display this singer's melody. fill the bars with even crotchets, then experiment — the following would be possible

bar 1 | bars 2, 3, 5, 6 | bar 4 | bar 7 | bar 8

  - Think positively about the words in relation to the time and rhythm: for instance, in bars 5 & 6 the words *bare* and *mute* gain emphasis from being lengthened by dots and *the* at the ends of these bars benefit from being shortened by tails. In bar 8 *very* is obviously two quavers, and *suit* will be a minim.

  - The quaver rest in bar 4 gives a small breathing space

  - Clap it and say the words; get the bars mathematically correct. Set out all 8 bars clearly with the rhythmic pattern faintly pencilled above the bars (as shown)

• Planning the melody (see *Compose a melody*   p.94)

Bellman's Song "Cold December"

• With this possible version in front of you, study the words and imagine the singer
  guess he's happy in his job
  he likes singing, but not too high – low – fast
  he's sorry for the poor man – all poor men
  he's looking forward to his tea

• Play the song, notice the following points
  • Choice of key — B minor
      minor suits the mood of the words
      the pitch of a complete octave in B minor is in a comfortable range to sing
  [NOTE: to work in any key you need jottings: B minor / key sig F♯ C♯ /
  tonic triad (i) B D F♯ / rel. major D triad D F♯ A / scale notes B C♯ D E F♯ G A(♮) B
  useful triads (ii) C♯ E G, (iv) E G B, (v) F♯ A♯ C♯]
  • Choice of notes
    bars 1 & 2: both bars start on the keynote and use the same notes
      repetition suits the 'stomping along' style of the song
      key is firmly established (keynote starts, 3 out of 4 notes are from the tonic triad)
    bars 3 & 4: both bars have sad-sounding words
      in a minor key the 6th degree of the scale can achieve a sad effect. It has been
      used to stress the word 'poor' and again the word 'clothen'd'. This is a strange
      word — 2 notes (6th & 5th degrees) have been slurred over the first syllable.
      This gives an appoggiatura-type accent (on the 6th degree again) to emphasise
      the word and add to the pathos of the phrase. 'Thin' is the last word in the first
      half of the song, so the dominant is used, followed by a quaver rest for the
      singer to take a breath.
    bars 5 & 6: in these two bars *sequential phrases* have been used (see p.94)
      in bar 5 "the trees are. . ." uses notes of the relative major triad
      in bar 6 "the birds are. . . " uses notes of the supertonic triad (triad (ii))in each
      bar the shape and the intervals are the same: 3rd down, perfect 4th up
      the use of sequential phrases supplies ongoing continuity
    bar 7: stepwise whole tones — one down, one up — move purposefully to —
    bar 8: three dominants and a tonic — no mistake — glad to be home!

  • Performance directions: study what has been suggested. Decide why these choices
    have been made.

A MODAL MELODY for an instrument or to an original lyric

• Play these modes, followed by the two melodies

Aeolian mode (white notes A-A)

Wraggle Taggle Gypsies

Three gyp-sies stood at the cas-tle gate: they sang so high, they_ sang so low. The

la - dy sate in her cham-ber late — her heart it melt-ed a-way like snow.

Dorian mode (white notes D-D)

*Greensleeves

* This well known mid 16th Century tune is often altered nowadays into the key of D minor, B♭ (key signature) in bars 2 and 10: C♯ (leading note) in bars 6, 7, and 14

• Experiment with white note chords — add 3rds (a). Invent your own.

(a)   (b)

• find chords which will follow each other effectively

• they may suggest melodic shapes which they could accompany (b)

• choose the mode you want (p.62) play it, shape the notes into phrases, give them a pattern and rhythm. Experiment with chords which will blend in. They can be used to
  • strengthen notes which need it (important words, first beats)
  • repeat a steady beat (like a foot tapping, or drum beat)
  • resound through a line of notes (like a colour wash behind a line drawing)

• as your melody takes shape you may prefer to do without chords

- **Original Lyric** — if this is your intention, write it first: your words will require certain rhythms and suggest certain phrasing when you come to write the melody. Draft out your ideas — subject matter, mood and style, metre, line-balance, rhyme (or not) . . .

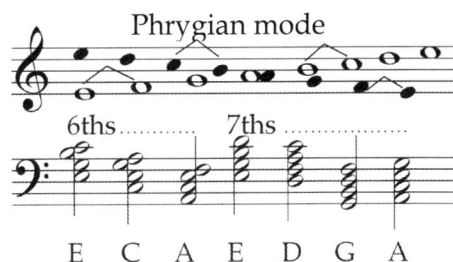

Phrygian mode

'The more you said' Study the lyric:

You said 'bye' — you said 'see you, bye' — you said
'It won't be long, I won't be far away . . .'
So you said 'bye, again' . . . You said
'the time will fly, I'll soon be back,
we'll keep in touch, I'll tex you ev'ry day . . .'
The more you said, the more I minded,
the more you said — the more you said the more I minded. } *repeat*

Play the mode - up & down
Play some triads and chords
with added 6th & 7th

Observations
- the song is about a person glad to be going away, and someone sad about it
- 'bye', 'see you', 'bye again' mean virtually the same thing
- 'it won't be long', 'the time will fly' etc. impersonal, ordinary phrases
- the words 'you said' are used repeatedly
- the two final lines keep harping on one obsessive idea

Creative ideas
- 'bye', 'see you' suggest longish notes 'by -e' 'see you'

- dots and tails for the casual cliché-type phrases; skipping along, happy and jaunty, keen to be gone — need cheery bits of tune

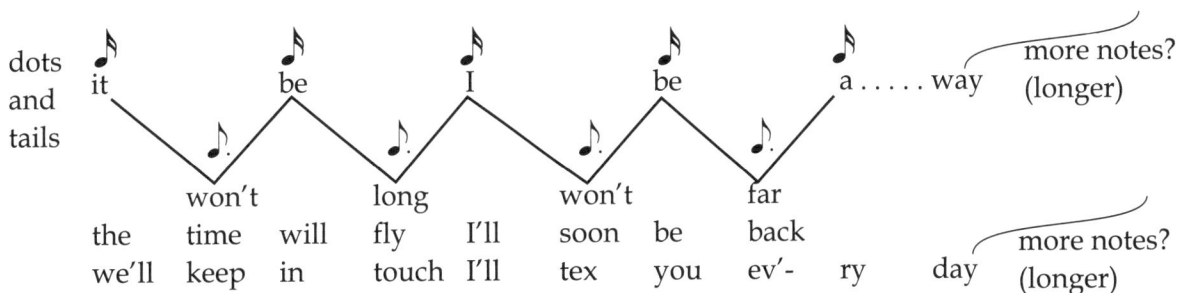

- 'the more you said, the more I minded' — emotionally charged phrases — need extra rhythmic and melodic emphasis to stress the pathos and gain sympathy. (If two singers, this section could be sung along in thirds)

- Setting of "The more you said" over the page. Play and study the vocal line then pay attention to the accompaniment. Be aware of the choices which have been made, and why.
  Perform it with somebody if you can.

The more you said

A song in the Phrygian mode

Modéré animé

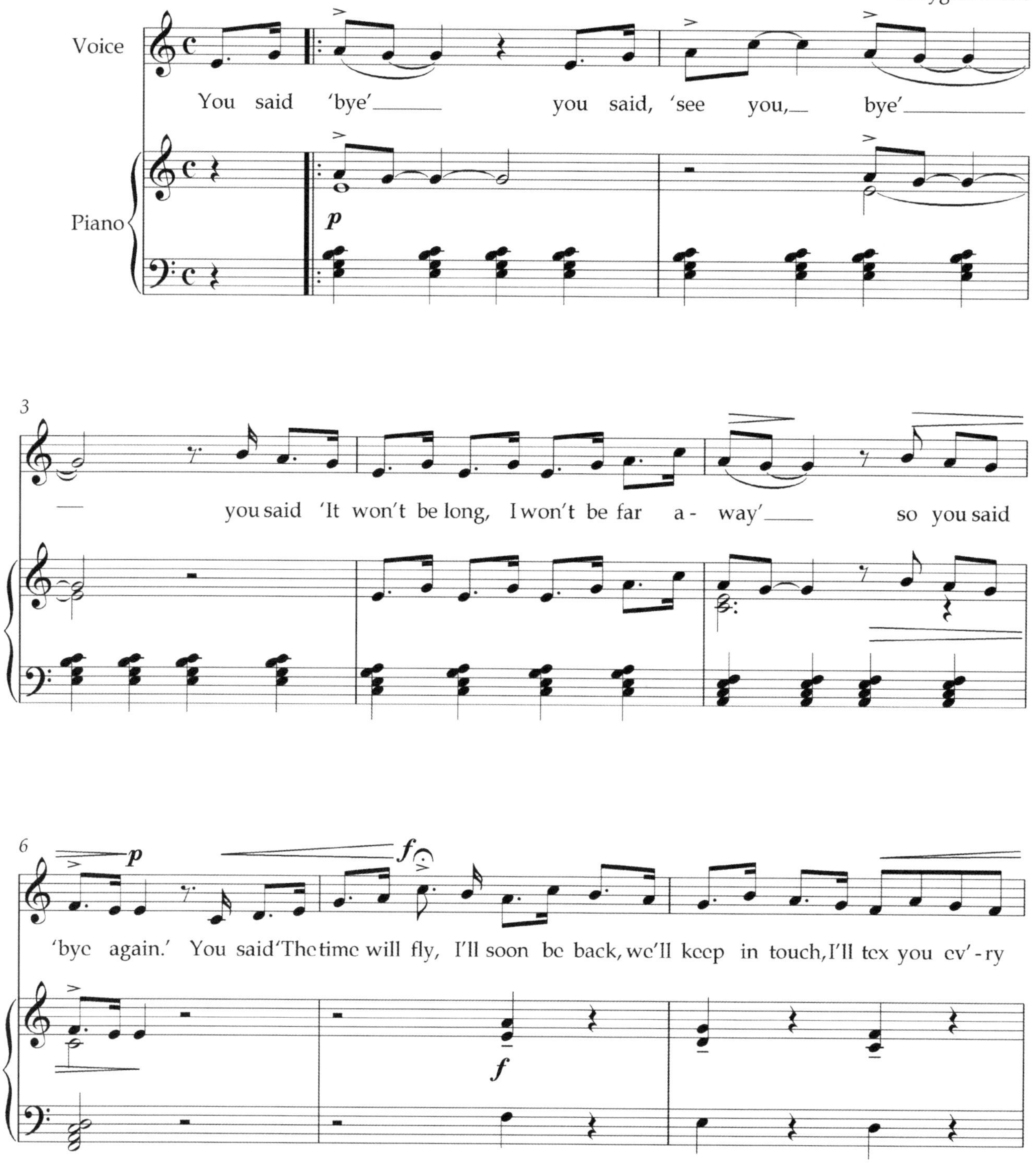

2

9 **en retenant** **plus lent**

day.' The more you said, the more I mind-ed: the more you said, the more I

14

mind-ed: the more you said, the more I mind-ed: the more you said — the more you

18 [1.] **a tempo**

said, the more I mind - ed. You said,

20 [2.] **cédez**

said, the more I mind - ed.

COMPOSING SONGS TO GIVEN WORDS

Questions: Compose melodies, using not more than 8 bars, to the following words. Write each syllable under the note or notes to which it is to be sung. Also indicate the tempo and other performance directions as appropriate.

"Shine out fair sun with all your heart,
Show all your thousand-coloured light."   *anon*

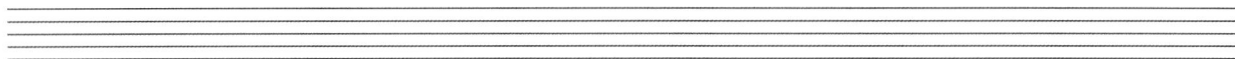

words _____

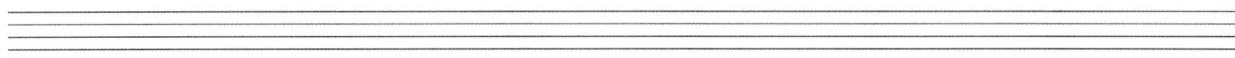

words _____

"When frost and snow are both together,
Sit by the fire and spare shoe-leather."   *traditional*

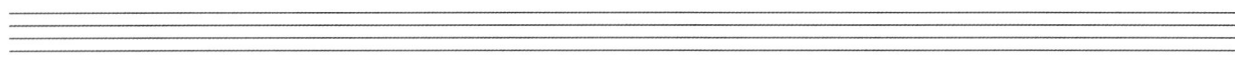

words _____

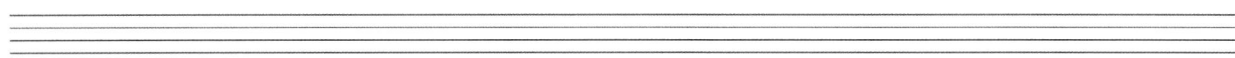

words _____

"A speckled cat and a tame hare
Eat at my hearthstone and sleep there."   *W. B. Yeats*

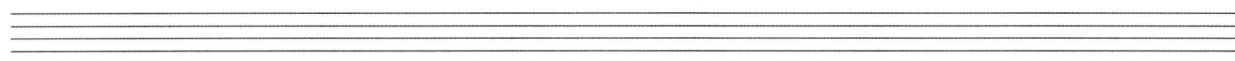

words _____

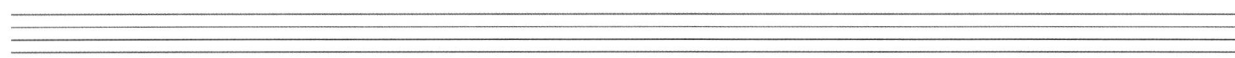

words _____

SONGS — CONTINUED

"There came two angels out of the East—
The one brought Fire, the other Frost."   *trad., treatment for a burn or scald*

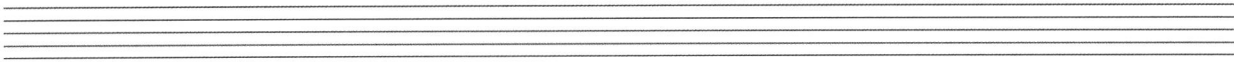

words _____

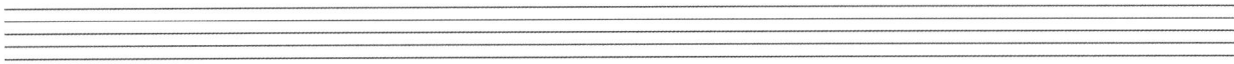

words _____

"Needle to needle and stitch to stitch —
Will you pull that old woman out of the ditch."   *Country lore;*
                                                          old knitting pattern

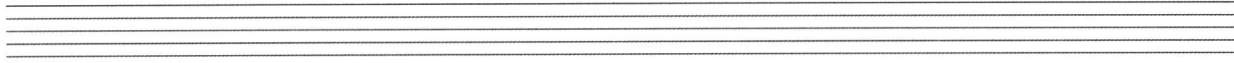

words _____

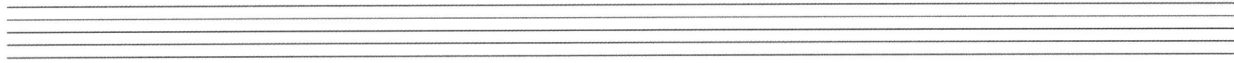

words _____

COMPOSING MELODIES FOR GIVEN INSTRUMENTS

Questions: Use the following openings to compose melodies, not more than 8 bars long, written for one of the given instruments. You may substitute a different clef if it is more suitable for your chosen instrument. Performance directions (tempo, phrasing, bowing, dynamics etc) should be included. Name your chosen instrument.

Instrument . . . .

oboe
trumpet
or horn

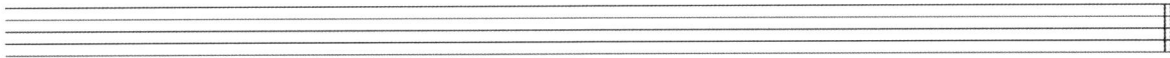

Instrument . . . .

violin
oboe or
classical guitar

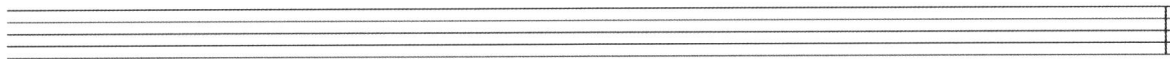

instrument. . . . .

cello
trombone
or bassoon

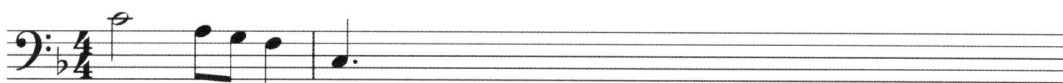

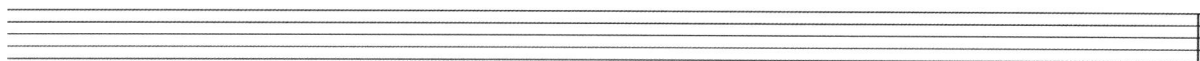

instrument. . . . .

viola
clarinet
or horn

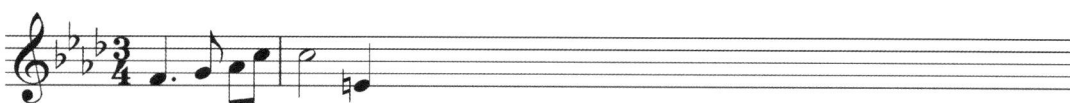

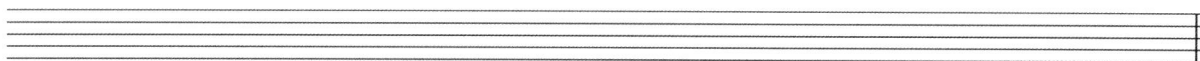

instrument. . . . .

violin
flute or
recorder

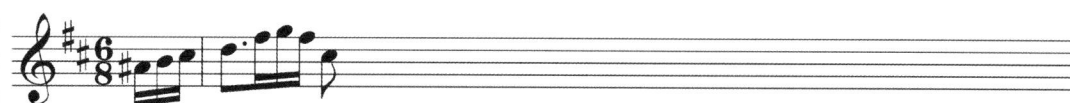

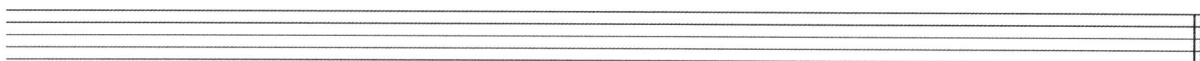

instrument. . . . .

bassoon
cello or
double bass

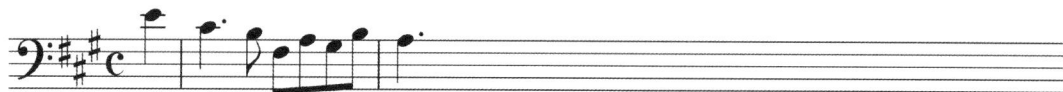

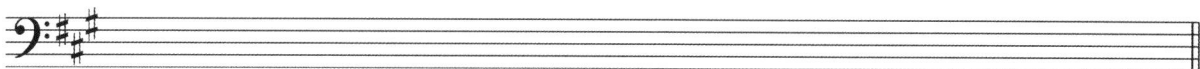

OBSERVATION and GENERAL MUSICIANSHIP

Sarabande
from suite *Auf die mayerin*

J. J. Froberger

- Name the ornament used in this sarabande . . . .
- Comment on the rhythmic structure — repetitive patterns, number of bars forming a unit. Comment on the placing of the ornament within this rhythmic framework

- Comment on the style and tonal ranges. Suggest a century when the music could have been composed.

- Fully describe the time signature. . . . . What is the beat note? . . . .
- Name three other courtly dances in the formation of a suite

- Suggest an Italian word or phrase suitable to indicate the style and speed required for the performance of a sarabande

- Bars 11 and 12 — modulation via . . . . . . (accidental) to key . . . .
- Bars 13 to 16 — modulation via . . . . . . (accidental) to key . . . .
- Bars 17 to the end: all accidentals abandoned, the music is once more in its home tonic key of . . . .

from **9 Variations on a Galliarde by John Dowland**

Samuel Scheidt
1587-1654

Theme: bars 9-12 (end)

Variation 2: bars 9-12 (end)

Variation 6: bars 9-12 (end)

1.   Soprano part Theme and Variation 2.
     - Comment on the difference between the 2 sections _____

     _____

     - Comment on the similarities _____

     _____

2.   All parts. Variation 6. Describe the change of texture _____

     _____

3.   Tenor and Bass parts. State in which sections and in which bars

       - Tenor is moved to treble stave _____
       - Bass has more notes than all the other parts_____
       - Comment on the similarities in the bass parts between theme / variations

4.   Alto part.
       - In which bar is the alto written in the bass clef? _____
       - In which section does the alto part have fewest notes? _____

5.   In your manuscript book rewrite the 4 bars of the theme for S. A. T. B. in open score

Opening of 2nd movement: Piano Sonata in C maj (hob XVI21)

Josef Haydn

- Insert the missing time signature. Describe the kind of time (simple, duple etc)

- add a rest in the bass clef, bar 2, to correspond to the time-value of the 13 note group

- Name the key of this extract

- describe the opening chord, also the chord between both hands in bar 5. Indicate their positions

- Legato phrase, bar 4: describe which (a) or (b) of the following volume directions is more appropriate (a) ───────   (b) ───────   Answer _____

- Name the ornaments in bars 4 ─────────── and 5 ───────────

  What does the sharp signify under the first ornament in bar 5?

- Would you encourage the use of the sustaining pedal in performing this style of music? Answer *yes* or *no*, and give a reason.

- Copy out the first 4 bars in your manuscript book observing all details and directions for performance

- Suggest a suitable metronome mark for this piece

from Josef Haydn — English Sonata — Hob XVI, 50

1st movement

3rd movement

1st movement

- The old French word *'harpègement'* was used to describe how the first three chords should be played. Find an English alternative description _____

- Draw the note and ornament above it to replace the 4 demi-semiquavers at the end of bar 1. Include the ♯

- There are 3 successive melodic 7ths in this extract. Find them; one is different from the other two: state whether 1st, 2nd, or 3rd — and how it is different. _____

- What key is this movement in? Do any of the accidentals in these four bars indicate a modulation? Answer *yes* or *no* _____ If yes, what is the new key indicated? _____

3rd movement

- Name the ornament in bar 3

- Find a place in this short extract where the chord indications $\begin{smallmatrix} 6 \\ 4 \end{smallmatrix}$ $\begin{smallmatrix} 5 \\ 3 \end{smallmatrix}$ would be appropriate. Insert them below the chords: explain their meaning

from String Quartet op. 51 no 2 *by* Johannes Brahms

- In what key is this movement? _____

- What instrument is *Bratsche* the German for? _____

- What does *mezza voce* mean? _____

- What do the slurred dots ⁀·· over the triplets mean to string players? _____

- Indicate two phrases (bar numbers) where all 4 players would use *exactly* the same bowing and tonal shaping? _____

- Give chord names and positions at A _____   B _____   C _____

- *Between the two violin parts*, give the full names of these intervals:
  bar 4, beat 1 _____   bar 6, beat 1 _____   bar 7 beat 3 _____

  bar 9, beat 3 _____   bar 13, beat 3 _____

- Suggest a suitable metronome speed for this minuet _____

- From your observation of the speed, style, texture, and overall dynamic level, underline the more suitable descriptive performance directions.

  martellato e strepitoso   or   *molto piangevole con espressione*

- Name 4 orchestral woodwind instruments which could play this music. List them in order from the top downwards _____

- In your manuscript book transcribe the alto clef part (line 3) from bar 8 to the end into the bass clef.

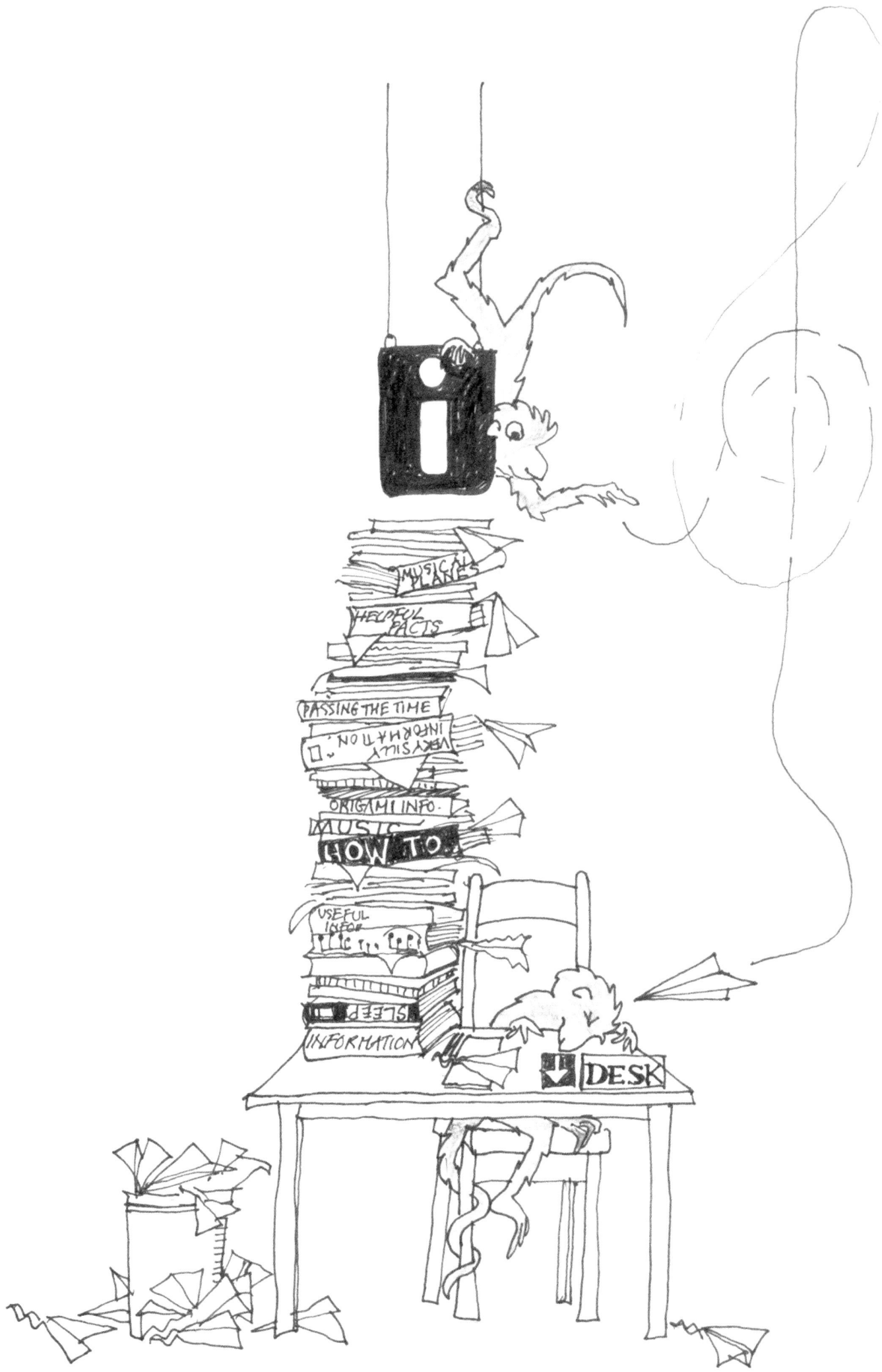

MUSICAL PLANES

HELPFUL FACTS

PASSING THE TIME

VERY SILLY INFORMATION

ORIGAMI INFO.

MUSIC

HOW TO.

USEFUL INFOR

SLEEP!

INFORMATION

DESK

A CAPELLA unaccompanied vocal music

ACCIACCATURA one-note ornament, sign ♪ (see p. 60)

ACCIDENTALS any sharps, flats or naturals indicated in a piece other than those in the key-signature

ALLEMANDE a German dance of moderate speed in 4 time (see also SUITE)

ALTO (contralto) — see VOICES)

ANACRUSIS the opening of a piece of music with a single up-beat or with several notes before a bar line; the time-value of the note(s) used must be subtracted from the final bar

APPOGGIATURA one-note ornament, sign ♪ (see p. 60)

AUGMENTED INTERVALS major or perfect intervals widened by a semitone (see Section IV Intervals)

AUGMENTED TRIAD one made up of two major thirds (see P. 43)

BAROQUE music written in the late 17th and early 18th centuries

BASS the lowest part in a composition (see VOICES)

BASSOON (see WOODWIND FAMILY)

BEAMING joining together by a line or lines or the stalks of similar notes which sub-divide larger notes, particularly beat notes (see Section II Time & Rhythm)

BOURRÉE A French dance in quick two-time, starting on an up-beat. (see also SUITE)

BOW the stick with horsehair stretched across used for playing string instruments

BOWING the signs V (up-bow) and ⊓ (down-bow) to indicate the direction in which the bow should be moved over the strings. Strong beats are often marked with a ⊓ sign. (see also SLURS)

BRASS INSTRUMENTS
(orchestral) Pitch ranges (written)

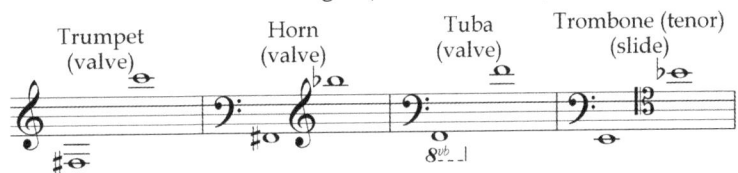

CADENCES formal use of certain chords to create a final, semi-final or unexpected effect at the endings of phrases. (see also FIGURED BASS (see pp. 51, 52))

CELLO (violoncello) see STRING FAMILY

CHORDS extensions of basic triads by doubling triad notes or by adding extra notes to enrich the sound, either in harmony or by dissonance

CHROMATIC **c. compositions** — music which uses many accidentals: **c. intervals** — when two notes forming a semitone have the same letter name. e.g. C - C♯: **c. scales** — all the steps are semitones (see p. 30)

CLARINET see WOODWIND FAMILY and TRANSPOSING INSTRUMENTS

C-CLEFS the name given to the alto and tenor clefs, which indicate the position of middle C on the stave (see p. 55)

CLEF the sign at the beginning of each stave which determines the position of the notes written on that stave. Most commonly used: the treble clef 𝄞 and the bass clef 𝄢:

COMPASS the pitch-range of notes covered by instruments or voices

COMPOUND INTERVAL an interval which is greater than an octave (see p. 40)

COMPOUND TIME the beat-notes are always dotted and therefore always divisible by three. The upper numbers of the **TIME SIGNATURE** are 6, 9, or 12 (see p. 20)

CON SORDINO (*pl.* **SORDINI**) an instruction to wind or string players to use the mute: to pianists, use the soft (left) pedal

CONCERT PITCH the standard by which orchestral instruments are tuned. A modern classical orchestra will tune to A = 440 Hz, meaning that the sound-wave produces by 440 vibrations per second is the A above middle C (violin A). Before a concert A is sounded by the oboe for other instruments to tune to; the oboe is chosen because its tone has the most penetrating quality

CONTRAPUNTAL relating to musical counterpoint; music written using interwoven melodic strands

COR ANGLAIS see **WOODWIND FAMILY** and **TRANSPOSING INSTRUMENTS**

CORNET see **TRANSPOSING INSTRUMENTS**

COURANTE (French) a running dance in 3-time. See also **SUITE**

DEGREES OF SCALE the numbered order, from 1 to 8, of scale notes

DIATONIC music using notes belonging in the key-signature without any extra chromatic notes

DIMINISHED INTERVALS minor or perfect intervals made smaller by a semitone (see pp. 34, 35)

DIMINISHED TRIADS triads made up of two minor thirds (see Section V Triads & Chords)

DOMINANT the 5th degree of the diatonic scale, always a perfect 5th from the tonic (see p. 30)

DOMINANT 7TH CHORD the addition of the 7th above a dominant root to the existing triad already using the 3rd and 5th above the dominant root, e.g. in key C — dominant G, 3rd B, 5th D, 7th F. The 7th is a minor interval and as a general rule should resolve onto the note below it (mediant). This allows the 3rd (leading note) to rise to the tonic

DOUBLE BASS (string bass) see **STRING FAMILY**

DOUBLE DOTTED NOTES notes with two dots beside them e.g. 𝅗𝅥.. The first dot is worth half the note, the second dot half the first dot e.g. 𝅗𝅥.. = 𝅗𝅥 + 𝅘𝅥 + 𝅘𝅥𝅮

DOUBLE SHARPS / FLATS sharp notes raise by a further semitone (sign ✕), flat notes lowered by a further semitone (sign ♭♭)

DUPLE TIME a time signature which denotes two beats in a bar e.g. $\frac{2}{4}$, $\frac{6}{8}$ The beats may be simple or compound (see p.20)

DUPLETS in compound time, where beats are sub-divided by three, a pair of notes used in place of the three. It is marked

DYNAMICS variations in volume during performance of a piece of music

ENHARMONIC EQUIVALENTS notes which sound the same as each other but are written as sharps rather than flats or vice versa e.g. F♯, G♯, A♯, can be written as G♭, A♭, B♭. Two major keys are enharmonic, G♭ (relative minor E♭) 6flats, and F♯ (relative minor D♯) 6 sharps

FIGURED BASS in four part harmony, if figures are printed below the bass notes they indicate the intervals to be used to form the chords above them

root position chords — no figures need be printed ($\frac{5}{3}$ taken for granted)

first inversion chords — 6 printed (3 taken for granted)

second inversion chords — $\frac{6}{4}$ always printed

cadential $\frac{6}{4}$ — the use of Ic (second inversion tonic) in the formation of cadences (see Section V Triads & Chords)

to form an imperfect cadence	Bass notes	Dominant $\frac{6}{4}$ or Ic	Dominant V	
to form a perfect cadence	Bass notes	Dominant * $\frac{6}{4}$ or Ic	Dominant V	Tonic I

* both the figures $\frac{6}{4}$ and the letter **c** by the Roman numeral mean the chord is a second inversion. Either may be used

FLUTE see **WOODWIND FAMILY**

FUGUE a polyphonic composition, for keyboard, orchestra or singers, of horizontally interwoven parts similar to a round. There are usually three, four or five 'voices'. Each in turn introduces the 'subject' — the main theme, often quite short. This is developed in different ways / by different means, including the introduction of counter-subjects.

FUNDAMENTAL TUNING A term applied to the construction of wind instruments. Some, e.g. clarinet, trumpet, horn, are built with dimensions that affect the tuning and cause the fundamental ("the note produced by the vibration of the whole of a sonorous body" *Shorter Oxford Dictionaryl*) to sound lower or higher than concert pitch. Other orchestral wind instruments e.g. flute, oboe, bassoon, trombone, are built with fundamentals tuned to concert pitch. See also **TRANSPOSING INSTRUMENTS** (see p.56)

GAVOTTE (French) a moderately animated dance in simple quadruple time. The phrases always begin on the third beat of the bar . See also **SUITE**

GIGUE a piece, usually in binary form, finale of a suite. Possibly English in origin. See also **SUITE**

GROUND BASS a short melodic figure repeated in the bass without variation, e.g. Pachelbel: Canon

GUITAR a 6 stringed plucked instrument of Spanish origin. The strings are tuned up from E in perfect 4ths except between the 4th and 5th string where the interval is a major 3rd. The fingerboard is fretted

HARMONIC   h. minor scales: the scale as indicated by the minor key signature, except for the raised leading note (see p. 26). h. intervals: written with the notes one above the other

HARMONICS   secondary sounds which can be produced by any note played, e.g. by slightly touching the strings of a string instrument or by over-blowing a wind instrument

HARPÈGEMENT (French, lit. "harp-like") the playing of chords on the piano with the notes rapidly following each other as in an arpeggio rather than in a block. The sign is

HARPSICHORD a keyboard instrument with one or more manuals; the strings are plucked to produce the sound. Universally used in the 16th, 17th and 18th centuries, now much used in performing early music. See also KEYBOARD INSTRUMENTS

HORN French — see BRASS INSTRUMENTS. TRANSPOSING INSTRUMENTS

INTERVAL   the size of the gap between two notes, or the difference in pitch between two notes. The two notes can be inverted e.g. C_D (a 2nd) becomes D_C (a 7th) (see p. 35)

INVERSIONS   re-arrangements of triads with the third or fifth in the bass rather than the root (see Section V Triads & Chords) The term inversion also refers to the turning upside-down or back-to-front of a theme, e.g. a fugue subject (see FUGUE)

KEYBOARD INSTRUMENTS   The history of their development has filled many books. Here are some of the details of the three most familiar::

pianoforte   Three memorable dates: 1709 Christofori, working in Florence, publicised his invention of the *hammer action* which enables pianists to control the speed of the hammer as it strikes the string, and thus to control the volume of sound produced. His Italian name for the instrument meant 'soft-loud'. 1783 John Broadwood, building pianos in London, devised the mechanism of the *sustaining pedal*, which lifts the dampers away from the strings, allowing resonance in sympathy with those already struck; this greatly enriches the sound. 1856 after years of pioneering work in America on the design of *iron frames*, the first Steinway grand piano was built in Boston, Massachusetts. The total string tension or "pull" on the frame of a modern grand piano can be as much as 30 tons: a wooden-framed instrument would be laid in ruins while being strung up.

organ   The sounds are made by air pumped (nowadays electrically) through different-size pipes ranging in length from 2 inches to 32 feet. Stops bring these pipes into action or shut them off. There are usually two, sometimes three manuals (keyboards) and a range of foot-pedals. Unlike the piano, where a note will die away even though a key is held down, organ notes maintain the same volume until the key is released.

harpsichord   The strings are plucked by *plectra* (quills). The volume can be varied a little using different sets of quills. Pedals can bring in extra-sounding strings and there are small felt dampers attached to the quills. All strings resonate until vibrations cease.

KEY SIGNATURE   the group of sharp or flat signs appearing after the clef on each stave, indicating the key (see p. 25)

LEADING NOTE   the 7th degree of a diatonic scale, a semi-tone step below the 8th (tonic) (see p.30)

MEDIANT   the third degree of a diatonic scale. In major scales a major third from the tonic, in minor scales a minor third (see p. 30)

MELODIC   **m. minor scales**: the form of minor scale in which the 6th and 7th degrees, although flattened by the key-signature, are raised by accidentals on the up scale. The down scale conforms to the key-signature (see Section III Scales & Keys); **m. intervals**: written with the notes sounding one after another as in a melody (see p. 26)

METRONOME a small machine invented in 1814 by Mälzel which emits an audible and visible beat at a pre-selected speed per minute. M.M. ♩ = 60 means that a crotchet beat lasts one second. Some metronomes can also sound note A at concert pitch (440 Hz). See also SPEED DIRECTIONS

MINUET a stately dance in 3-time, often followed by a second minuet called a Trio. See also SUITE

MODULATION using accidentals in order to change key(s) temporarily during a piece of music e.g. in sonata form development sections. Often many related keys are briefly suggested (see p.59)

MORDENT a two-note ornament, signs ⚬ (see p. 60)

MOVEMENTS separate sections of a continuous composition such as a symphony or sonata, always with differing speeds, sometimes in differing keys

MUSETTE a pastoral-type piece on a drone bass, sometimes linked to a gavotte in a dance suite. See SUITE

MUTE a device to reduce the volume of sound produced by an instrument

NEAPOLITAN SIXTH first inversion of the major triad formed on the flattened super-tonic (II) in a minor key. Normally it is followed by V then I. This progression sounds distinctive and memorable

OBOE See WOODWIND FAMILY

OCTAVE an interval encompassing the eight notes of the diatonic scale. The upper note has exactly twice the number of vibrations as the lower. **at the octave** — a term used in transposition, meaning to shift all the notes to be transposed up or down one octave

OPEN NOTES on wind instruments, those produced naturally as distinct from 'stopped' notes produced with the help of keys or valves; on string instruments, those not stopped by the left hand

OPEN SCORE music written for several parts, a separate stave for each part (see p. 54)

ORNAMENTS formal groups of small notes e.g. turns, trills, used to elaborate or accentuate rhythmic, melodic or harmonic aspects of a composition. (see p. 60)

PASSING NOTES non-structural notes in a melody not requiring specific chords to harmonise them

PEDAL POINT a device in composition whereby a single note, usually in the bass, often the dominant, is held for a considerable time or repeated while other parts continue to move freely

PERCUSSION INSTRUMENTS all instruments played by being struck

PERFORMANCE DIRECTIONS instructions on the copy regarding effective speed, volume, style etc. by the composer or editor

PHRASING refers to the style of a performance. Depending on the instrument (voice, violin etc.), it concerns breath control, bowing control; also dynamic, stresses, inflexions etc. In piano music phrases are marked ⌒ Similar lines in string music indicate SLURRED BOWING

PITCH the exact height or depth of any musical sound according to the number of vibrations which produce it

POLYPHONY the interweaving of two or more melodic strands so that they make musical sense

PRELUDE   originally an introductory piece, e.g. in BAROQUE dance suites, JS Bach's Preludes and Fugues. Later used for short romantic piano pieces, e.g. Chopin: Preludes

PROGRESSION (**chord p.**) the movement from one chord to the next, e.g. in forming CADENCES

RECORDER   woodwind instruments made in 4 different sizes giving different pitch ranges. The descant recorder is often used in school music

SARABANDE   a slow, stately dance in 3-time. See also SUITE

S.A.T.B.   stands for Soprano, Alto, Tenor, Bass, used in open and short scores, the letters printed to the left of the clef (see p. 54)

SEMITONE   in Western music the smallest interval between two notes (see p. 32)

SHORT SCORE   when four-part harmony is written on two staves, treble and bass, e.g. in hymn books: *soprano* (stalks up), *alto* (stalks down) in treble clef; *tenor* (stalks up), *bass* (stalks down) in bass clef

SIMPLE TIME   the beats are divisible by two. Beat-notes are indicated by the lower number of the time signature (see p. 16)

SLURRED BOWING   (string music) more than one note played in one bow movement

SLURS   (a) curved lines linking groups of notes which relate to each other to form phrases, especially in piano music; (b) signs for legato bowing in string music; (c) in vocal music, indicating one syllable to two or more notes. These must be included when setting words to music

SONATA FORM   (a basic outline of content and key structure – liable to much modification)
exposition *first subject* — tonic key (major or minor). Cadence in dominant; *second subject* — dominant or relative major. Cadence in this key at the double bar.
development section of subject matter, modulating through related keys back to the . . .
recapitulation *first subject* — in tonic. Cadence in tonic. *second subject* — in tonic, leading to end of movement in tonic
Throughout the movement the two main subjects are developed by subsidiary themes and linked by bridge passages

SOPRANO   see VOICES

SPEED DIRECTIONS

Italian	English	metronome
largo	very slow	40 - 52
larghetto	faster than largo	54 - 66
adagio	slow	68 - 76
andante	at a walking (moderate) pace	78 - 108
moderato	moderate speed	110 -120
allegro	lively, usually fast	122 - 160
presto / prestissimo	quick, very fast indeed	162 - 200 / 200+

STALKS   for rules on the placing of note-stalks see Starters, page 12. For exceptions see SHORT SCORE

STAVE   a set of five lines carrying notes indicated by the clef

STRING FAMILY   the four members of this family are tuned as follows

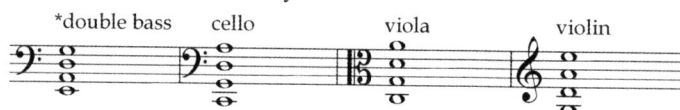

* music for the double-bass is written an octave higher than it sounds

SUB-DOMINANT the fourth degree of the diatonic scale, always a perfect 4th from the tonic (see p. 30)

SUB-MEDIANT the sixth degree of the diatonic scale, in major scales a major 6th from the tonic, in minor scales a minor 6th from the tonic (see p. 30)

SUITE early music collections of dances, usually including **ALLEMANDE, BOURRÉE, GAVOTTE, COURANTE, MINUET** (usually two), **SARABANDE, GIGUE.** Sometimes a **PRELUDE** is included, occasionally a **MUSETTE** follows the gavotte

SUPER-TONIC the second degree of the diatonic scale, always a major 2nd from the tonic (see p. 30)

TEMPO (Italian) speed of performance

TENOR see **VOICES**

TETRACHORD a group of four notes containing two tones and a semitone, in any order. It encompasses the interval of a perfect 4th (seepp. 25, 26)

TEXTURE a term indicating whether music is chordal, polyphonic, widely spaced over the stave, closely written etc.

TIES two or more notes of the same pitch linked together thus ⌢ . The values of the second and subsequent notes are added to the first

TIME SIGNATURE two figures, one above the other, indicating the number of beats and the value of the beat-note in each bar, printed on the top stave, or where there is a change of time during a piece (see pp. 16, 20)

TONIC the first degree of a scale. The keynote of a piece

TRANSCRIPTION often a quite free arrangement of a musical composition from what the composer intended. The term is also used to refer to re-writing music in a different clef (e.g. bass clef to tenor clef) while keeping the same pitch (see p. 55)

TRANSPOSING INSTRUMENTS e.g. clarinet, trumpet, cornet in B♭; clarinet, trumpet in A; horn, cor anglais in F. Scale of C: the letters (B♭, A, F) indicate the actual scales these instruments produce when playing the scale of C major: the first group sound the scale of B♭ (a whole tone lower). the second the scale of A major (a minor third lower), the third the scale of F major (a perfect fifth lower). When playing in an ensemble or orchestra, all the instruments need to sound at the same pitch (concert pitch). In order to correct these pitch differences, parts for transposing instruments are written, e.g. a whole tone up for B♭ instruments, a minor third up for instruments in A, a perfect fifth up for instruments in F. For transposing instruments in other keys the same system applies. See also FUNDAMENTAL TUNING (see p. 56)

TRANSPOSITION re-writing music in a different key (See pp. 55, 56)

TRE CORDE (instruction to pianists) stop using the soft pedal

TRIAD a three-note chord (see Starter p. 11)

TRILLS see **ORNAMENTS** (see p. 60)

TRIPLE TIME a time signature which denotes three beats in a bar. It may be single or compound e.g. $\frac{3}{4}$ $\frac{9}{8}$ (see pp. 16, 20)

TRIPLET in simple time, where beats are divisible by two, a group of three notes replacing two. They are marked thus (see p. 68)

TRITONE an interval made up of three whole-tones

TROMBONE see BRASS INSTRUMENTS

TRUMPET see BRASS INSTRUMENTS, TRANSPOSING INSTRUMENTS

TUBA see BRASS INSTRUMENTS

TURN see ORNAMENTS (See p. 60)

UNA CORDA (instruction to pianists) use the soft pedal

VIOLA see STRING FAMILY

VIOLIN see STRING FAMILY

VOICES

WOODWIND FAMILY pitch ranges (written)

§ Cor anglais music is written in the same range as oboe but sounds a perfect fifth lower (e.g. C to F)

* transposes up one octave from printed notes

† single reed

‡ double reed

MUSICAL TERMS IN COMMON USE

Unhurried movement, smooth, moderate

adagio	slowly
allegretto	more leisurely than allegro
andante	at a walking pace
andantino	faster than andante
grazioso	moving gracefully
larghetto	less slow than largo
largo	slowly
lento	slow
moderato	at a moderate speed
portamento	glide smoothly from one note to another
sostenuto	sustained
tenuto	held

GERMAN

langsam	slowly
massig	moderate speed

FRENCH

soutenu	sustained

Delicate style gentle sensitive touch

delicato	delicately
dolce	sweetly pleasant
dolcissimo	very pleasant
leggiero	lightly
pastorale	in a gentle pastoral style
piano(ø –issimo)	quiet playing
soave	gentle, smooth

FRENCH

doucement	gently
en dehors	prominent, emphasised
lointain	in the distance

GERMAN

ruhig	calm, peaceful
zart	delicate

Getting louder

crescendo	getting louder
più forte	more volume
rinforzando	increasing the tone

Getting quieter

calando	decreasing tone (and speed)
decrescendo	getting quieter
diminuendo	quieter
morendo	dying away
perdendosi	dying away
smorzando	tone diminishing

Melodic, expressive, sympathetic mood

cantabile	in a singing style
cantando	in a singing style
con anima	with deep feeling
dolente	sadly, with sorrow
dolore	sadly, with sorrow
espressione	expressively
espressivo	expressively
legatissimo	as smooth as possible
legato	smooth, joined
piacevole	pleasant, agreeable
piangevole	plaintively
semplice	simply
tempo rubato	with a flexible tempo
tenerezza	with tenderness
tranquillo	tranquil, peacefully

FRENCH

doux (très d. plus d.)	sweetly, loving

GERMAN

einfach	simply
süss	sweet(ly)
traurig	sadly

Getting slower, dying away, broadening out

allargando	broadening out
meno mosso	reduce speed now
rallentando	getting slower
ritardando	gradually slower
ritenuto	held back
slentando	gradually slower

FRENCH

cédez	give way
en retenant	gradually slower
retardé	slow up
trainé	decrease speed

Getting faster, speeding up after slowing down

a tempo	back to the original speed
accelerando	gradually faster
più animato	more animated
più mosso	more movement
stringendo	gradually faster
tempo primo	back to the first speed

FRENCH

animez	more animated
au mouvement	up to speed again
en pressant	hurrying

Fast, cheerful, detached, vigorous, neat and nimble, lively

allegro	lively
giocoso	merrily
presto(ø -issimo)	fast, very fast
scherzando	playfully
scherzo	a joke
spiccato	with a springing bow
spiritoso	spirited
staccato(ø -issimo)	detached
veloce	swiftly
vivace	quick, lively
volante	flying

GERMAN

bewegt	with movement
frölich	cheerful, frolicsome
lebhaft	lively
schnell, **-er**	quick, quicker

FRENCH

vite, **vif**, **vivement**	quickly

Stately, steady, dignified, usually slow

grandioso	in a grand manner
grave	slower, solemn
largamente	broadly
maestoso	majestically
marcia	like a march
martellato	hammered out
nobilmente	nobly
pesante	heavy, ponderous
risoluto	resolute, bold
ritmico	rhythmically
sonore	full-toned

GERMAN

breit	with breadth

FRENCH

marqué	stressed

Vigorous, agitated, passionate, plenty of movement

agitato	agitated
animato	animated
bravura	boldly, spirited
brillante	brilliant(ly)
con brio	with vigour
con forza	forcefully
con fuoco	with fire
energico	with energy
forte, ¢ -issimo	loud, very loud
furioso	with fury
impetuoso	impetuously
marcato	accented, marked
passionato	passionately
sforzando	forcing a sudden accent
spiritoso	with spirit

GERMAN

feurig	fiery

USEFUL LITTLE WORDS

ITALIAN

al fine	to the end
arco	the bow
assai	very
ben, **bene**	well
coda	short convincing ending
col, **colla**	with
come prima	as at first
con	with
da capo (**D.C.**)	back to the start
dal segno (**D𝄋**)	back to sign 𝄋
e, **ed**	and
legno	stick, bow
ma	but
meno	less
mezza voce	in an undertone
mezzo	half
molto	much
moto	movement
non troppo	not too much
più	more
poco	a little
sempre	always
senza	without
tacet	silent
tanto	much
tutti	all

FRENCH

avec	with
bémol (**le**)	the flat sign
dièse	the sharp sign
gauche	left (-hand)
m.d.(**main droit**)	right hand
m.g.(**main gauche**)	left hand
plus	more
sans	without
sec	dry
un peu	a little

GERMAN

aber	but	mit	with
B	*the note* B flat	moll	minor (key)
ein	one	nicht	not
etwas	somewhat	sehr	very
H	*the note* B natural	und	and
immer	constantly, always	voll	full
Lied	song	wenig	little, less
		zu	too

OTHER WORDS AND PHRASES COMMONLY USED

ad lib	at pleasure	pizzicato *pizz.*	(string players) pluck the strings
doppio movimento	twice as fast	prima volta	first time
fortepiano *fp*	loud then soft	quasi	as if, almost
G. P.	general pause	segue	(usually orchestral) go on to what follows
L'istesso tempo	same speed of beat, though beat notes have changed	simile	in a like manner
obbligato	an indispensable section, cannot be omitted	sotto voce	in an undertone
op., opus (Latin)	a work, a published composition	subito	suddenly
ossia	or (indicating an alternative version)	sul ponticello	(string players) play close to the bridge
ostinato	a frequently repeated section, often in the bass	tempo commodo	at a convenient speed
		tempo giusto	in exact time
pausa	a rest	tempo rubato	flexible handling of the timing
ped., pedal	(for pianists) use the right (i.e. sustaining) pedal	V.S. *volti subito*	(orchestral) turn over quickly
		vibrato	vibrate to modify the tone.

MUSICAL TERMS (alphabetical list)
(G = German, F = French)

a tempo	back to the original speed	calando	decreasing tone (and speed)
accelerando	gradually faster		
adagio	slowly	cantabile	in a singing style
agitato	agitated	cantando	in a singing style
allargando	broadening out	cédez(F)	give way
allegretto	more leisurely than allegro	con anima	with deep feeling
		con brio	with vigour
allegro	lively	con forza	forcefully
andante	at a walking pace	con fuoco	with fire
andantino	faster than andante	crescendo	getting louder
animato	animated		
animez (F)	more animated	decrescendo	getting quieter
au mouvement(F)	up to speed again	delicato	delicately
		diminuendo	quieter
bewegt (G)	with movement	dolce	sweetly pleasant
bravura	boldly, spirited	dolcissimo	very pleasant
breit(G)	with breadth	dolente	sadly, with sorrow
brillante	brilliant(ly)	dolore	sadly, with sorrow

doucement(F)	gently	**piangevole**	plaintively
doux (très d. plus d.)(F)	sweetly, loving	**piano(ø –issimo)**	quiet playing
		piu animato	more animated
einfach (G)	simply	**piu forte**	more volume
en dehors(F)	prominent, emphasised	**piu mosso**	more movement
en pressant(F)	hurrying	**portamento**	glide smoothly from one note
en retenant(F)	gradually slower		to another
energico	with energy	**presto(ø -issimo)**	fast, very fast
espressione	expressively		
espressivo	expressively	**rallentando**	getting slower
		retardé(F)	slow up
feurig (G)	fiery	**rinforzando**	increasing the tone
forte, ę -issimo	loud, very loud	**risoluto**	resolute, bold
frölich(G)	cheerful, frolicsome	**ritardando**	gradually slower
furioso	with fury	**ritenuto**	held back
giocoso	merrily	**ritmico**	rhythmically
grandioso	in a grand manner	**ruhig(G)**	calm, peaceful
grave	slower, solemn		
grazioso	moving gracefully	**scherzando**	playfully
		scherzo	a joke
impetuoso	impetuously	**schnell, -er(G)**	quick, quicker
		semplice	simply
langsam (G)	slowly	**sforzando**	forcing a sudden accent
largamente	broadly	**slentando**	gradually slower
larghetto	less slow than largo	**smorzando**	tone diminishing
largo	slowly	**soave**	gentle, smooth
lebhaft (G)	lively	**sonore**	full-toned
legatissimo	as smooth as possible	**sostenuto**	sustained
legato	smooth, joined	**soutenu (F)**	sustained
leggiero	lightly	**spiccato**	with a springing bow
lento	slow	**spiritoso**	spirited
lointain(F)	in the distance	**spiritoso**	with spirit
maestoso	majestically	**staccato(ø -issimo)**	detached
marcato	accented, marked	**stringendo**	gradually faster
marcia	like a march	**süss(G)**	sweetly
marqué(F)	stressed		
martellato	hammered out	**tempo primo**	back to the first speed
massig (G)	moderate speed	**tempo rubato**	with a flexible tempo
meno mosso	reduce speed now	**tenerezza**	with tenderness
moderato	at a moderate speed	**tenuto**	held
morendo	dying away	**trainé(F)**	decrease speed
		tranquillo	tranquil, peacefully
nobilmente	nobly	**traurig(G)**	sadly
passionato	passionately	**veloce**	swiftly
pastorale	in a gentle pastoral style	**vite, vif, vivement(F)**	quickly
		vivace	quick, lively
perdendosi	dying away	**volante**	flying
pesante	heavy, ponderous		
piacevole	pleasant, agreeable	**zart(G)**	delicate